The Age of Colonialism

Other titles in the World History Series

The Age of Colonialism

Don Nardo

LUCENT BOOKS
An imprint of Thomson Gale, a part of The Thomson Corporation

Detroit • New York • San Francisco • San Diego • New Haven, Conn. • Waterville, Maine • London • Munich

© 2006 Thomson Gale, a part of The Thomson Corporation.

Thomson and Star Logo are trademarks and Gale and Lucent Books are registered trademarks used herein under license.

For more information, contact
Lucent Books
27500 Drake Rd.
Farmington Hills, MI 48331-3535
Or you can visit our Internet site at http://www.gale.com

LIBRARY OF CONGRESS CATALOGING-IN-PUBLICATION DATA

Nardo, Don, 1947–
     The age of colonialism / by Don Nardo.
       p. cm. — (The world history series)
     Includes bibliographical references and index.
       ISBN 1-59018-833-0 (hard cover : alk. paper) 1. Colonies—History—Juvenile literature.
2. Imperialism—History—Juvenile literature. 3. Great Britain—Colonies—History—
Juvenile literature. 4. Europe—Colonies—History—Juvenile literature. I. Title. II. Series.
     JV105.N37 2006
     325'.341—dc22
                                                                          2005027901

Printed in the United States of America

Contents

Foreword

Each year, on the first day of school, nearly every history teacher faces the task of explaining why his or her students should study history. Many reasons have been given. One is that lessons exist in the past from which contemporary society can benefit and learn. Another is that exploration of the past allows us to see the origins of our customs, ideas, and institutions. Concepts such as democracy, ethnic conflict, or even things as trivial as fashion or mores, have historical roots.

Reasons such as these impress few students, however. If anything, these explanations seem remote and dull to young minds. Yet history is anything but dull. And therein lies what is perhaps the most compelling reason for studying history: History is filled with great stories. The classic themes of literature and drama—love and sacrifice, hatred and revenge, injustice and betrayal, adversity and overcoming adversity—fill the pages of history books, feeding the imagination as well as any of the great works of fiction do.

The story of the Children's Crusade, for example, is one of the most tragic in history. In 1212 Crusader fever hit Europe. A call went out from the pope that all good Christians should journey to Jerusalem to drive out the hated Muslims and return the city to Christian control. Heeding the call, thousands of children made the jour-ney. Parents bravely allowed many children to go, and entire communities were inspired by the faith of these small Crusaders. Unfortunately, many boarded ships captained by slave traders, who enthusiastically sold the children into slavery as soon as they arrived at their destination. Thousands died from disease, exposure, and starvation on the long march across Europe to the Mediterranean Sea. Others perished at sea.

Another story, from a modern and more familiar place, offers a soul-wrenching view of personal humiliation but also the ability to rise above it. Hatsuye Egami was one of 110,000 Japanese Americans sent to internment camps during World War II. "Since yesterday we Japanese have ceased to be human beings," he wrote in his diary. "We are numbers. We are no longer Egamis, but the number 23324. A tag with that number is on every trunk, suitcase and bag. Tags, also, on our breasts." Despite such dehumanizing treatment, most internees worked hard to control their bitterness. They created workable communities inside the camps and demonstrated again and again their loyalty as Americans.

These are but two of the many stories from history that can be found in the pages of the Lucent Books World History series. All World History titles rely on sound research and verifiable evidence, and all give students a clear sense of time, place, and chronology through maps and time-lines as well as text.

All titles include a wide range of authoritative perspectives that demonstrate the complexity of historical interpretation and sharpen the reader's critical thinking skills. Formally documented quotations and annotated bibliographies enable students to locate and evaluate sources, often instantaneously via the Internet, and serve as valuable tools for further research and debate.

Finally, Lucent's World History titles present rousing good stories, featuring vivid primary source quotations drawn from unique, sometimes obscure sources such as diaries, public records, and contemporary chronicles. In this way, the voices of participants and witnesses as well as important biographers and historians bring the study of history to life. As we are caught up in the lives of others, we are reminded that we too are characters in the ongoing human saga, and we are better prepared for our own roles.

1492
Sailing for Spain, Italian-born mariner Christopher Columbus lands in the West Indies, initiating the age of colonialism.

1543
Polish astronomer Nicolaus Copernicus publishes *On the Revolutions*, in which he asserts that Earth revolves around the sun.

1625
The French establish a colony at St. Domingue in the Caribbean to exploit sugarcane and other cash crops.

| 1500 | 1550 | 1600 | 1650 | 1700 |

1555
Michelangelo completes the sculpture *Pietà* in Florence.

1756–1763
Years of the Seven Years' War, in which Britain, France, and their allies fight for world dominance.

1607
English settlers land at Jamestown, Virginia, the first of Britain's American colonies.

the Age of Colonialism

1776
Britain's thirteen American colonies declare their independence, marking the beginning of worldwide resistance to colonialism.

1884–1885
The European powers meet in Berlin to facilitate the subjugation and colonization of Africa.

1858
Britain imposes direct rule on India, its most valuable colony.

1905
German American physicist Albert Einstein publishes his ground-breaking special theory of relativity.

1750 **1800** **1850** **1900** **1950** **2000**

1914–1918
Years of World War I, in which Britain, France, the United States, and their allies fight Germany, the Ottoman Empire, and their allies.

1970
The United Nations outlaws colonialism.

1929
The stock market collapses, eventually leading to the Great Depression.

1947
India gains its independence from Britain.

1756
Composer Wolfgang Amadeus Mozart is born.

1939–1945
Years of World War II, in which the Allies defeat Germany, Italy, and Japan.

The Failure to Learn from History

"Those who cannot remember the past are condemned to repeat it,"[1] wrote the twentieth-century American philosopher George Santayana. He meant that people who do not recognize and learn from the mistakes made by those who came before them will inevitably make the same mistakes. And the danger exists that this destructive process will continue to repeat itself indefinitely. Thus, history is not simply a collection of facts about the past that are studied in school and soon forgotten. History is, at least in part, a blueprint for how to act and react in the present and the future.

The Controllers and the Controlled

Perhaps nowhere has the truth of Santayana's maxim been demonstrated more clearly than in the long history of colonialism and imperialism. Today these terms are often used interchangeably, even by historians and other scholars. However,

the experts do sometimes distinguish between the two terms. They generally define *colonialism* as direct political control and rule imposed by a nation on a distant piece of territory. That territory, called a colony, may or may not receive large numbers of settlers from the mother country. Examples include the colonies Britain established in Massachusetts, Virginia, and Jamaica in the 1600s, in New Zealand in 1841, and in Nigeria in 1914.

Technically, *imperialism* is a somewhat more general concept relating to the creation and maintenance of empires. An imperialistic nation exercises its power and influence over distant cities, islands, and/or countries, which collectively make up its empire. It does this through economic means, the threat of force, armed intervention, or a combination of these. Some of the subject states might be colonies settled and directly ruled by the mother country. Others might retain some form of self-rule but be economically dependent on and largely do the bidding of the mother country. In the 1800s, for instance, Britain used its powerful navy to maintain a vast global empire. That empire included colonies and dependent territories in India, Ceylon (now Sri Lanka), Singapore, Africa, the Pacific Ocean, and elsewhere.

Thus, colonialism and imperialism are so closely interrelated that it is no wonder the two concepts have become largely synonymous. It is difficult to discuss one without discussing the other. Yet technical distinctions between colonialism and imperialism were irrelevant to the people who lived in the many colonies and subject states of the past. For each of these outposts, the stark reality was the relationship it had with the mother country. That relationship ultimately boiled down to two basic elements or groups—the controllers and the controlled.

Today, with the benefit of hindsight, the major inherent weakness of such a system seems obvious. The controlled are always dependent on and beholden to the controllers, who make all the important decisions. The system can work for an indefinite period, especially when the controllers' decisions are beneficial to the controlled. But sooner or later, as a matter of human nature, the controlled will come to believe that they should have the right to make those decisions for themselves. And they will rid themselves of their controllers in whatever way they can.

For Americans, the most vivid and memorable example of this scenario began with Britain's colonization of eastern North America in the 1600s. Eventually colonial opposition to the policies of the mother country brought about the American Revolution, which ended British rule and created the United States. But Britain's loss of its American colonies turned out not to be an isolated case. In the years that followed, Britain and several other great powers encountered resistance to their imperial systems and policies all over the world. Often these powers had started out with good intentions, and in some cases their efforts had helped the populations they controlled. But more often the controlled peoples had been exploited and had come to yearn for independence.

American literary critic and philosopher George Santayana asserted that people often ignore the past.

In this woodcut, American colonists protest the Stamp Act in the 1760s, one of the series of events that led to the American Revolution.

Meanwhile, the mother countries found that they had to spend more and more money and resources to maintain control, until doing so became a burden. These trends reached a climax in the mid-twentieth century, when all the colonial empires established by prominent European nations between the late 1400s and early 1900s finally fell apart. In the words of noted American historian Louis L. Snyder:

> The imposition of European civilization on backward peoples, the outthrust of the white man's civilization,

had some beneficial results . . . [including] improvement of living conditions and the development of native commerce and industry. But in other cases the living conditions of the natives were depressed rather than improved. Individuals in the colonizing countries often made enormous profits, but the average citizen gained little more than the pleasure of pointing to little colored splotches on the map as "our colonies." Imperialist policies necessitated the maintenance of strong military and naval forces, which means higher and higher taxes.[2]

Not surprisingly, therefore, over time colonialism and imperialism came to be seen in a decidedly negative light by both the controllers and the controlled.

The Lesson of Ancient Empires

In retrospect, more striking than the breakup of the early modern European empires was the fact that they had formed in the first place. In large degree this occurred because the European powers did not learn the lessons of their own history. Most of the nations of Europe developed from small medieval kingdoms. And most of these kingdoms were originally established by the so-called barbarian peoples who caused the fall of the Roman Empire in the fifth and sixth centuries.

Before their realm declined, the Romans built the largest and most successful empire the world had yet seen. At its height, in the second century, it encompassed the entire Mediterranean region and most of southern Europe, as well as Britain, North Africa, and large sections of the Near East (now called the Middle East). At the time, the Romans—including both those in charge and average people—could not imagine that they would someday be unable to hold their empire together. Like other successful peoples in history, including the British in the 1700s and 1800s and many Americans today, they naively imagined that their society would exist indefinitely, perhaps forever.

The Romans also ignored the lessons and fates of the empires that had preceded theirs. Some of Rome's subject territories in the Near East had once been part of the Persian Empire, for example. The Persians, too, had once controlled a vast realm made up of diverse peoples and cultures. And, in turn, that realm had been built on the wreckage of prior empires, including those of the Medes and Assyrians.

Modern Rounds of Colonialism

Just as the Persians failed to learn from the mistakes of past imperialists and the Romans ignored the fate of the Persian realm, early modern Europeans did not pay heed to the blunders and fates of all the ancient empires. When Christopher Columbus, an Italian sailing for Spain, arrived in the islands of the West Indies in the late 1400s, a new round of empire-building began. In what has come to be called the Age of Colonialism, Spain, Portugal, England, France, the Netherlands, and others scrambled for pieces of North and South America and eventually set their sights on Africa and southern Asia as well.

Then, after nearly three centuries of redrawing the global map and exploiting native peoples, the colonial movement slowed considerably in the late 1700s. With the major exception of the British, Snyder points out, "enthusiasm for acquiring colonies abated . . . [and] many decried [such activities] as [a] wasted effort."[3] But those who thought that the great powers had at last learned from the mistakes of the past were soon sorely disappointed. In the decade of the 1870s, the age of colonialism resumed with a vengeance. In a new scramble to exploit territory, riches, and less-developed peoples, the United States, Turkey, and Japan joined the Europeans. And once more the maps changed, particularly those of Asia, Africa, and the Middle East.

In 1492 Christopher Columbus and his crew claim the West Indies as Spanish territory, initiating the first great age of colonialism.

U.S. bombers strike Baghdad during the 2003 invasion of Iraq. Many Muslims saw the assault as a modern example of imperialism.

Only in the mid-twentieth century did the colonial powers begin to see that, in the long run, maintaining self-serving empires was detrimental to both themselves and the peoples they controlled. These empires dissolved, and their dependent parts were replaced by independent, sovereign nations. Aiding in this momentous transition was the United Nations (UN), established at the conclusion of World War II. In 1970 the UN went a step farther and declared colonialism illegal.

Yet considering the trends and events of thousands of years of human history, some people wonder whether colonialism and imperialism are truly gone for good. For example, large numbers of people in various parts of the world worry about U.S. intervention in Iraq, which began in 2003. They see the American presence in that country and other sectors of the Middle East as the beginning of a new and troubling round of imperialism. Others strongly disagree with this assessment, viewing U.S. efforts in that region as part of a global war on terrorism.

What people on both sides of the argument can agree on is that the free peoples of the world must be ever vigilant. They must try to ensure that no powerful and ambitious nation tries to build an empire to enrich and empower itself at the expense of less powerful countries. The question is how long such vigilance will be maintained and to what degree people will resist the colonialist-imperialist impulse when it eventually resurfaces. There can be little doubt that it will do so. That, after all, is a lesson that history has repeatedly taught and that people can no longer afford to ignore.

Chapter One

The First Great Age of Colonialism

As a convenient generalization, historians often date the modern age of colonialism (as opposed to colonialism in ancient times) from the late 1400s to the mid-1900s. In that span of roughly five centuries, Spain, England, France, and several other European nations became ardent imperialists. Seeking to expand their power and influence, they sent explorers to find unknown territories around the globe and claimed those lands as their own. They then proceeded to exploit these colonies, along with any native peoples who inhabited them. The colonial empires expanded. But over the course of time the mother countries encountered increasing difficulties in governing and maintaining their distant possessions. Eventually, they lost or granted independence to their colonies.

Scholars frequently divide this long, complex age of expanding and contracting empires into shorter, more manageable time periods. The first began in the late 1400s and lasted a bit more than two centuries. Because it witnessed Europe's discovery and initial explorations of North and South America and other regions, it is often called the Age of Exploration. Hundreds of colonies were established during this period, so phrases such as "the first great era of colonialism" are also used to describe it.

Whatever the age is called, it proved to be a pivotal turning point in world history. In a sense, it was a sort of historical bridge over which Europe passed from medieval times to the modern era. For countless centuries, Europeans had been confined more or less to their own neighborhood, along with parts of western Asia, and were isolated from large sections of the world. But exploration and colonization of vast new lands filled with natural resources provided the raw materials for rapid and enormous economic growth and political and military expansion. This allowed a handful of small European nations to impose their wills and cultures on large portions of the globe. As the American historian William H. McNeill puts it:

> Once they had mastered [the] dangerous waters [of the Atlantic Ocean], European sailors found no seas impenetrable, nor any ice-free coast too formidable for their daring. In rapid succession bold [ship] captains sailed into distant and hitherto unknown seas. . . . The result was to link the Atlantic face of Europe with the shores of most of the Earth. What had always been the extreme fringe of [the European sphere] became, within little more than a generation, a focus of the world's sea lanes, influencing and being influenced by every human society within easy reach of the sea. . . . The sheltering ocean barrier between the Americas and the rest of the world was suddenly shattered and . . . the key to world history from 1500 [on] is the growing political dominance first of western Europe, then of an enlarged European-type society planted astride the north Atlantic.[4]

Columbus's three small ships cross the Atlantic in 1492. The Age of Exploration that followed helped usher in the modern era.

Columbus Describes Hispaniola

Among the islands Columbus discovered in the West Indies were Cuba, which he called Johana, and Hispaniola, which he called Hispana. In his first report intended for Queen Isabella (quoted in Bernard and Hodges's Readings in European History *), he described Hispana in ways that made it sound appealing as a place to establish a colony.*

There are very lofty and beautiful mountains, great farms, groves and fields, most fertile both for cultivation and for pasturage, and well adapted for constructing buildings. The convenience of the harbors in the island, and the excellence of the rivers . . . surpass human belief, unless one should see them. In it, the trees, pasturelands, and fruits differ much from those of Johana. Besides, this Hispana abounds in various kinds of spices, gold, and metals. The inhabitants of both sexes of this and of all the other islands I have seen . . . always go naked as they came into the world, except that some of the women cover parts of their bodies with leaves or branches or a veil of cotton.

This woodcut shows the natives of Hispaniola greeting Columbus, who saw the island as ripe for colonization.

"God, Glory, and Gold"

The desire for political dominance, as McNeill suggests, was certainly one of the underlying motives for the colonial expansion of Spain, France, and other European realms. But other motives were more fundamental and driving, at least at first. The traditional, familiar adage is that they formed a trilogy—"God, glory, and gold." *God* refers to the desire, indeed the perceived responsibility, to convert so-called heathen peoples living in the newly discovered lands to Christianity. And *glory* means the increased prestige of a colonizing nation and its leaders.

But these and other motives for the colonizing movement, though important, took a decided back seat to the third element of the old adage. *Gold* is another way of saying economic factors, including not only gold, silver, and other precious metals but also land, timber and other raw materials, and lucrative trade in spices, fabrics, slaves, and other valuable commodities. Simply put, the quest for wealth was key because the wealthiest countries are almost always the most powerful, influential, and prestigious.

To acquire wealth as quickly as possible, Europe's colonizing nations at first employed an economic theory and system that came to be known as mercantilism. In essence, its practitioners saw the distant colonies as having a twofold purpose and value. First, they were rich sources of raw materials. A mother country could mine those materials, bring them back to its homeland, and there use them to manufacture a wide range of products. Some of these products would be used within the mother country. But others would be exported back to the colonies, whose inhabitants would pay high prices for them, thereby further enriching the mother country. "Those who advocated mercantilism," Duke University scholar John W. Cell points out,

believed that exports to foreign countries were preferable both to trade within a country and to imports because exports brought more money into the country. They also believed that the wealth of a nation depended primarily on the possession of gold and silver. Mercantilists assumed that the volume of world wealth and trade was relatively static, so one country's gain required another's loss. According to this view, a colonial possession should provide wealth to the country that controlled it. Colonies were not supposed to compete with the mother country's home industries. Empires were closed systems, designed to keep competitors out.[5]

Imperial Spain

The Spanish were the first Europeans to create such a large-scale closed economic system based on the acquisition of overseas colonies. Their neighbors, the Portuguese, had been the first Europeans to exploit the Canary Islands and other islands lying near Europe's western coasts. But the Spanish were the first to cross the Atlantic and establish permanent colonies in North and South America. (Some evidence shows that the Vikings made a few settlements in what is now southeastern Canada a few hundred years before the arrival of the Spanish; but these outposts did not last long and had no significant effect on European history.)

The crucial initial landfall in North America, of course, occurred in 1492 when Christopher Columbus arrived in the West Indies (now the Caribbean islands). An

Italian, Columbus had managed to acquire ships and backing from Isabella, queen of the Spanish kingdom of Castile. He had sailed west in hopes of reaching and establishing trade with India and other regions of southeastern Asia, collectively called the Far East. Moreover, Columbus thought nothing of conquering and exploiting native peoples whose technology and weapons were far less advanced than those possessed by himself and other Europeans. One typical entry from his log begins with a benign, quite complimentary description of the natives but then matter-of-factly states, "They do not bear arms, and do not know them. . . . They have no iron. Their spears are made of cane. . . . They would make fine servants. . . . With fifty men we could subjugate them all and make them do whatever we want."[6]

Like Columbus, Isabella and later Spanish leaders viewed the newly found lands and peoples across the sea strictly as commodities to be exploited. These leaders readily grasped the potential economic benefits for their country and sent out other explorers, soldiers, and colonizers. "In an amazingly brief period of time," McNeill writes, the Spanish "proceeded to explore, conquer, and colonize the New World with extraordinary energy [and] utter ruthlessness."[7] In fact, by the end of the 1500s, Spain had managed to gain full or partial control of Florida, Cuba, Mexi-

Like many other Europeans who followed them in the Americas, the Spanish cruelly killed or enslaved most of the natives they encountered.

Portuguese Maritime Innovations

In this excerpt from his book The Rise of the West, *historian William H. McNeill explains how some crucial contributions made by the Portuguese, especially a nobleman who became known as Prince Henry the Navigator (1394–1460), made Europe's first great age of exploration and colonialism possible.*

Europe's maritime supremacy was [profoundly aided by] . . . the efforts of Prince Henry the Navigator and his successors. . . . Prince Henry brought to Portugal some of the best mathematicians and astronomers of Europe, who constructed simple astronomical instruments and [mathematical] tables by which ship captains could measure the latitude of newly discovered places along the African coast. . . . The new methods . . . allowed the Portuguese to make usable charts of the Atlantic coasts. . . .

At the same time, Portuguese naval experts attacked the problem of improving ship construction. [They] rapidly improved seaworthiness, maneuverability, and speed of Portuguese and . . . other European ships. . . . Other innovations allowed a crew to trim the sails to suit varying conditions of wind and sea, thus greatly facilitating steering and protecting the vessel from disaster in sudden gales.

Portugal's Henry the Navigator shares the latest maps of the coasts of Africa with his men.

co, Panama, Venezuela, and numerous other regions of the Americas.

In this way, the Spanish created the largest of the early European overseas empires. It was also one of the most profitable. The Spanish mined gold and silver, exploited and exported native slave labor, and established a plantation system to produce sugarcane and other raw materials. By about 1550, less than sixty years after

Columbus's first voyage, Spain was collecting some 303 million pesos (equivalent to many millions of dollars today) from its mercantile system of overseas colonies. By 1600, that number had reached 2.7 billion pesos and was still rising.

The Portuguese Head East

Spain would surely have reaped even higher profits had it not been for major competition from other colonial powers, at first particularly Portugal and the Netherlands. At the time, these were very small countries with minimal populations. But their modest size belied their importance in world political and economic affairs.

In fact, the Portuguese might well have beaten Spain to the Americas had Portuguese leaders not committed a crucial error in judgment. In 1484, well before he approached Queen Isabella, Columbus asked Portugal's King John II for ships to cross the Atlantic and establish trade relations with the Far East. But John and his advisers were convinced that the best way to reach that region was to sail southeastward around Africa and then cross the Indian Ocean. So Columbus went to the Spanish, who ended up benefiting greatly for backing him.

Nevertheless, Portugal's exploration and exploitation of the eastern route to the Far East did prove quite profitable in the long run. The Portuguese established valuable colonies and trading posts in the Azores and on Africa's western coast in the early to mid-1400s. Then Portuguese navigator Bartholomew Dias sailed around the Cape of Good Hope, on Africa's southern tip, in 1488. Only nine years later, another Portuguese explorer, Vasco da Gama, made it all the way to India. And in the years that followed, Portugal set up trading posts there, as well as on the coasts of China and Japan. Later, following Spain's lead in the Americas, the Portuguese also colonized Brazil, which eventually became Portugal's most valuable colony, producing huge profits in sugarcane, coffee, and slaves.

The Enterprising Dutch

The success of Portuguese trading efforts in the Far East is all the more remarkable considering the strength of the competition. Although the Dutch began exploiting the area somewhat later, they rapidly caught up and became major players in Europe's growing mercantile enterprise. Part of the reason the Netherlands was able to achieve this success was that it had become a financial powerhouse. By 1600 that country, though tiny, had cornered the shipping and banking markets within Europe itself. Thus, the Dutch could well afford the considerable initial expenses of setting up overseas trading posts and colonies.

To oversee this huge operation, in 1602 a group of formerly competing Dutch companies pooled their resources and formed the Dutch East India Company. Its avowed goal was to dominate the spice trade in southeastern Asia. To this end, the company established a foreign headquarters at Batavia (now Jakarta), in what is now Indonesia. The company also built numerous small but well-fortified coastal colonies throughout Southeast Asia. The enterprising Dutch early made the decision not to waste resources on the creation of large, populous settlements. By concentrating on sea trade, rather than administering large tracts of countryside, they were able to maximize their profits.

To further streamline the operation, the Dutch East India Company sent only essential personnel, which at the time were all men. As University of California scholar Eric A. Jones explains:

Virtually no European women accompanied the men to the area . . . so the men married or cohabitated with Asian women . . . and their children were raised as Asians. . . . [Thus] the Dutch never represented more than a small percentage of the population in their own settlements, which resembled contemporary Asian port-states. Even so, the Dutch were far and away the most significant European presence in seventeenth-century Asia, sending some 978,000 people there . . . and

This eighteenth-century painting depicts a major Dutch trading post in the 1660s. Such posts sprang up all over the Far East.

returning with more shipping tonnage than Portugal, England, [and] France . . . combined.[8]

Britain's Jewel in the Crown

As Jones points out, Britain and France also attempted to compete for markets in the Far East. An important milestone for the British was the formation of the British East India Company in 1600. This organization concentrated most of its money and energies in developing a colonial presence in India. That presence consisted of numerous plantations, factories, and supply depots, as well as small towns and forts to maintain them. The leading local products exported to England included fine cotton and silk as well as large quantities of tea, dyes, and spices.

The British also took the wise step of convincing local Indian leaders to help British colonists and merchants import and export goods. In 1615 King James I sent a top diplomat, Sir Thomas Roe, to negotiate with the emperor Jahangir, who then controlled approximately 70 percent of India. In exchange for rights to build colonies and use Indian ports, Roe promised Jahangir a steady inflow of English-made luxury goods. Very pleased with this arrangement, the Indian ruler wrote to King James, saying in part:

[With] the assurance of your royal love, I have given my general command to all the kingdoms and ports of my dominions to receive all the merchants of the English nation as the subjects of my friend [i.e., James]. In what[ever] place they [the English colonists] choose to live, they may have free liberty without any restraint. And [at] what[ever] port they shall arrive, neither Portugal nor any other [nation] shall dare to molest their quiet. And in what[ever] city they shall have residence, I have commanded all my governors and captains to give them freedom answerable to their own desires, to sell, buy, and to transport [Indian products] into their country at their pleasure. For confirmation of our love and friendship, I desire Your Majesty to command your merchants to bring in their ships of all sorts of [English-made] rarities and rich goods fit for my palace.[9]

Thanks in part to such cooperation from Indian authorities, Britain's enterprise in India became immensely successful. Indeed, the British eventually came to see India as the "jewel in the crown" of their overseas empire.

Meanwhile, the British were just as successful in their colonization of North America. On what is now the eastern seaboard of the United States, numerous British colonies sprang up, among them Jamestown, Virginia, in 1607; Plymouth, Massachusetts, in 1620; Massachusetts Bay in 1632; and New York, a former Dutch colony (New Netherlands), which the British captured in 1664. Farther north, the British settled Newfoundland beginning in 1610. And far to the south, a string of islands stretching from the tip of Florida to the northern coast of South America became the British West Indies. These islands, many of which were taken from the Spanish, supported large sugar plantations that maintained huge annual exports.

British colonists land at Jamestown, Virginia, in 1607, one of many British overseas colonies established in the seventeenth century.

Instructions on How to Build a Colony

In 1607 a group of English colonists established the Virginia Colony, or Jamestown. Their sponsor, the Virginia Company, gave them a list of instructions (excerpted here from the Web site of the Avalon Project of the Yale Law School) explaining how to choose a site for the colony as well as how to build it and plant crops.

You shall do your best endeavor to find out a safe port in the entrance of some navigable river, making choice of such a one as runs farthest into the land. . . . When you have made choice of the river on which you mean to settle . . . make selection of the strongest, most wholesome and fertile place. . . . You must take special care that you choose a seat for habitation that shall not be overburdened with woods near your town. For all the men you have shall not be able to cleanse [clear] twenty acres a year. Besides that, it may serve as a [hiding place] for your enemies round about. Neither must you plant [your crops] in a low or moist place, because it will prove unhealthful. . . . It [is] necessary that all your carpenters and other such like workmen . . . build your storehouse and [other public structures] before any house be set up for any private person.

The French in North America and Africa

The French were even more successful than the English and the Spanish in the production of sugarcane in the Americas. In 1625 the French established the colony of St. Domingue (later called Haiti) in the western sector of the large Caribbean island of Hispaniola. The colony became the biggest single exporter of sugarcane in the hemisphere. In fact, St. Domingue, which also produced coffee, cotton, and tobacco, proved to be one of the most valuable European colonies in the entire world.

The French also colonized the North American mainland. They were especially successful in the Great Lakes region and St. Lawrence River valley. In 1608, in what is now southern Canada, French explorer and geographer Samuel de Champlain founded the colony of Quebec. Nearby Montreal was established in 1642. The chief natural resource exploited in this region was animal furs, which fetched high prices in Europe. Farther south, the French claimed possession of much of the Mississippi River valley, which would come to be known as the Louisiana Territory.

An important French colony also was established in Senegal, on the western coast of Africa. First settled in 1624, it later became a major stopping point for captors transporting black slaves to the Americas. In this first age of colonialism, French and other European exploitation of Africa was confined mainly to coastal regions. Most of the interior regions of the so-called dark continent would be claimed by the European powers in a later burst of colonial activity.

Meanwhile, the first spate of European colonialism had succeeded in changing the face of the globe in an astonishingly short time span. When Columbus departed from Spain on his three small ships in 1492, Europeans did not know that North and South America and numerous other distant lands even existed. Yet by the early 1700s, virtually all of these territories had been claimed and/or colonized by the leading European powers. At the time, no one could have guessed that some of these colonies would some day become independent nations both richer and more powerful than the nations from which they had sprung.

Chapter Two

The Challenges of Running a Colony

The manner in which the European powers administered and managed their far-flung colonies varied from place to place and time to time. This was partly because of differences in culture and philosophy among the colonizing nations themselves. But to a greater degree it stemmed from the fact that some colonists had different goals and approaches than others. Thus, several different kinds of colonial entities sprang up across the globe.

One of the more common types of colony is sometimes referred to as a colony of settlement (or settlement colony). As the name suggests, the main emphasis was on setting up towns and farms and, in effect, transferring a small piece of the mother country to a foreign locale. This inevitably resulted in the colonists pushing aside, and in some cases exterminating, any native populations they encountered. For the most part, colonies of settlement were located in temperate zones having climates similar to that of Europe. Britain's Ameri-

can and Canadian colonies are well-known examples.

Also common were colonies of exploitation. They are also called tropical dependencies because they were often located in tropical regions where plentiful warmth and sunshine supported large plantations. The emphasis in these colonies was on producing large quantities of cash crops, such as sugarcane, spices, or cotton. Such colonies attracted few permanent settlers and were populated mainly by merchants, wealthy planters, and soldiers for security. Because the colonists needed cheap labor to work the plantations, they generally did not kill or displace the natives but instead exploited them. Many such colonies existed in the Caribbean and Indonesian regions.

Other kinds of colonies were less common but no less important to the mother countries. India, for example, was a pre-existing empire that already had a sophisticated economy when parts of it became a colonial entity administered by Britain. In a very different case, Cecil Rhodes, leader of Britain's Cape Colony, invaded a neighboring region without British backing. The territory he seized and colonized became known as Southern Rhodesia (today the nation of Zimbabwe). Such colonies, which form independently or even in defiance of the mother country, are sometimes called contested settlement colonies.

Despite these differences in goals and physical setup, all of the overseas colonies had some important similarities. First, each had some kind of connection to a powerful European nation populated and ruled by white Christians. Second, each colony faced the challenges of administering itself and staying economically profitable. Finally, each colony had to deal with the local natives, which often turned out to be the biggest challenge of all.

Colonial Administration

Next to dealing with the natives, the most daunting challenge European colonists

The Cuban sugar plantation depicted in this woodcut was one of many tropical dependencies that Europeans established in the West Indies.

faced was administering or ruling their respective local territories and populations. The approaches used to govern colonies varied widely according to local conditions. But a few basic models emerged and were widely imitated among a majority of the colonies of settlement and colonies of exploitation.

For example, the administrative systems of many settlement colonies roughly resembled those in Britain's American colonies. Most of these started out with charters, documents that granted the colonists the authority to settle in an area and set down some basic rules and guidelines for organizing the colony. These charters were issued either by the British government or by a company licensed by the government.

In time, the colonists went beyond these initial blueprints and set up local governments that were in many ways miniature versions of Britain's national government. Each colony had a chief executive—the governor—who was appointed by the British king. And each had a legislature made up of a group of well-to-do, influential colonists. The first colonial American legislature was Virginia's House of Burgesses, established in 1619. Like Britain's national legislature, Parliament, the Burgess-

The initial meeting of the House of Burgesses, in Virginia in 1619, marked the first time that an elected legislature met in the Americas.

The British King Calls the American Colonists Rebels

These are excerpts from the August 23, 1775, proclamation (quoted in volume one of Commager and Morris's The Spirit of Seventy-Six*) issued by King George III, in which he officially declared that Britain's American colonies were in a state of rebellion.*

Many of our subjects in divers[e] parts of our Colonies and Plantations in North America, misled by dangerous and ill-designing men, and forgetting the allegiance which they owe to the power that has protected and supported them . . . have at length proceeded to open and avowed rebellion, by arraying themselves in a hostile manner . . . and traitorously preparing, ordering, and levying war against us. [Therefore] we have thought fit . . . to issue our Royal Proclamation, hereby declaring, that . . . [British soldiers and civilians] are obliged to exert their utmost endeavors to suppress such rebellion, and to bring the traitors to justice.

es and other colonial assemblies could make laws and thus enjoyed a measure of self-government. But local colonial authority was limited because a colony's governor could veto any law enacted by the local legislature.

One reason that colonies of settlement were so often governed in similar fashion to their mother countries was the makeup of their populations. At first, they consisted mainly of white people transplanted from those countries. So most of a colony's residents felt entitled to many of the same rights they or their parents had enjoyed in the mother country.

In contrast, most colonies of exploitation had mainly nonwhite populations from the start. The highly profitable French colony of St. Domingue was a clear example. When French planters took control of the region in the late 1600s, they immedi-

ately began exploiting black slaves, some of whom had been imported earlier by the Spanish, as a workforce. By the late 1700s, the colony supported some 28,000 whites of French ancestry, a roughly similar number of mulattos (people of mixed race), and a staggering 455,000 black slaves.

Here, as in many other colonies of exploitation, civil rights and government participation were determined largely by race. The whites, who made up only a small proportion of the population, were the only ones with full rights. And only a fraction of the whites took part in local government. There was a local assembly dominated by a handful of wealthy planters, but its authority was limited by two local officials—a military governor and a civilian administrator—both appointed by the French government.

In St. Domingue and colonies like it, administrative and policy decisions, both in the colony and in the mother country, were based mainly on economic considerations. The bottom line was future profits. In contrast, in settlement colonies such decisions also took into account the future growth, security, and happiness of a large, permanent white society.

Differing Economic Challenges

Still, economic prosperity was as important in settlement colonies as it was in non-settlement colonies. The different kinds of colonies simply faced some different economic challenges and employed appropriately different methods to meet those challenges. Both colonies of settlement and colonies of exploitation began by concentrating on one or a few basic raw materials, of which precious metals, timber, wool, sugarcane, spices, tea, and coffee were generally the most important. In the mercantile system, mother countries grew rich from distributing products manufactured from these materials.

But over time the settlement colonies grew larger, more populous, more diverse, and more in need of a wider variety of products to sustain themselves. As John W. Cell puts it, their economies

> came to resemble those of European nations. Their agriculture diversified, and they developed [their own] manufacturing industries. Because most settlement colonies gained political self-rule early, they could use protective tariffs (taxes on imports) to shelter their young industries. These industries could grow without com-

petition from more advanced industries in other countries. The result was high-wage labor and a high standard of living . . . for white settlers. [10]

Inevitably, therefore, most of the colonies of settlement diverted more and more of the resources they produced to their own uses and eventually became self-sufficient. Able to thrive on their own, they became less and less dependent on their mother countries. They often developed feelings of cultural and political separateness as well. These factors partially explain why many of the residents of Britain's American colonies eventually felt justified in resisting British rule.

The economic situation in colonies of exploitation, such as those in the West Indies and in Indonesia, was quite different. Their white populations were small and generally part of a ruling elite of planters and merchants. They funneled most of their money into the upkeep of their lucrative plantations.

At the same time, the white planters and merchants saw no need nor felt any obligation to invest in good housing or other amenities for the poor natives and/or slaves. Scholars often refer to the latter groups, which did almost all of the menial labor, as the subsistence sector of the colony. The subsistence sector employed "the bulk of the population and produced most of the food that fed them," Cell explains.

> The subsistence sector was inefficient, had little investment, paid poor wages, and supported a low and often declin-

ing standard of living. Its food production failed to keep pace with the country's rising population. Because the [planters and merchants] provided few health benefits or other kinds of social security (such as assistance for the unemployed, the elderly, or people with disabilities), the subsistence sector absorbed much of the cost of raising children and caring for sick or old people. The subsistence sector thereby subsidized the relatively prosperous and advanced [planters and merchants].[11]

It is no wonder, then, that colonies of exploitation, such as St. Domingue, remained largely underdeveloped, both physically and economically, and dependent in many ways on the mother country.

Slaves harvest sugarcane on a West Indian plantation. Such slaves were routinely mistreated and lived in impoverished conditions.

A Colonial Slave Code

The use of slave labor was common in European colonies around the globe, and the government of each colony typically set down rules to regulate and control its slaves. The rules quoted here (from the Web site "Slavery at the Cape") were enacted by the Dutch in Cape Town, southern Africa, in 1754.

Slaves are to be indoors after 10 P.M. or carry a lantern at night. Thus, slaves are not permitted to be on the street at night after 10 P.M. without a torch. Slaves are not to ride horses nor wagons in the streets. Slaves are not to sing, whistle, or make any other sound at night. . . . Slaves are not to meet in bars, buy alcohol, or form groups on public holidays. Slaves are not to gather near entrances of a church during the time of religious services being conducted. . . . Slaves who insulted or falsely accused a freeman would be flogged . . . Slaves who struck a slaveholder were to be put to death. Slaves are not permitted to own guns or to carry dangerous weapons.

The "Inferiority" of the Natives

Settlement colonies unfairly exploited people, too, of course. Despite their diversified economies and advanced political systems, for instance, Britain's American colonies used slaves. One major difference was that settlement colonies tended to push out native peoples and import slave workers from somewhere else. By contrast, tropical dependencies like St. Domingue tended to keep the natives in the colony, put them to work, and import slaves only to replace dwindling supplies of natives.

Thus, approaches to dealing with the natives varied from colony to colony. However, one grim reality prevailed in all of the colonial entities established by the European powers. The white colonizers invariably believed that they were racially, intellectually, and morally superior to the natives. It was seen as only natural, therefore, for the whites to displace, enslave, or otherwise exploit native populations.

This arrogant attitude derived in part from a mistaken idea repeatedly accepted and misused throughout human history: Namely, those cultures that develop large cities and advanced technology must somehow be inherently superior to those that do not. This had been the so-called logic behind the ancient Greek and Roman characterization of the then-tribal, largely rural peoples of central Europe as "barbarians."

Similarly, early modern Europeans observed that most of the native peoples they encountered had little technology, no books or written laws, and lived under what the whites viewed as simple and primitive conditions. The vast majority of colonizers failed to see that native cultures were often just as complex and rich as European ones, though usually in less overt ways. Noted American historian Howard Zinn observes:

> Columbus and his successors were not coming into an empty wilderness, but into a world . . . where the culture was complex, where . . . the relations among men, women, children, and nature were more beautifully worked out. . . . They were people without written language, but with their own laws, their poetry, their history kept in memory and passed on [by oral means].[12]

European feelings of superiority also stemmed from deep-seated racism. White colonizers typically thought that the "primitive" and "backward" conditions in which most native peoples lived were due to the supposedly lesser intelligence of nonwhite races. In fact, throughout most of the colonial period a majority of Europeans readily accepted some variation of the view set

Spanish colonists brutalize native workers. The rationale for such cruelty was a belief that white Europeans were racially and morally superior.

forth by a French aristocrat, Count Arthur de Gobineau, in 1853. In his book, *The Inequality of Human Races*, he states:

The [black] variety [of human] is the lowest [of the races], and stands at the foot of the ladder. The animal shape that appears in the shape of the pelvis is stamped on the negro from birth, and foreshadows his destiny. His intellect will always move within a very narrow circle. . . . The [Asian] man has little physical energy, and is inclined to apathy. . . . His desires are feeble. . . . He does not dream or theorize. He invents little. We come now to the white peoples. These are gifted with . . . an energetic intelligence. . . . At the same time, they have . . . an extreme love of liberty. . . . [History] shows us that all civilizations derive from the white race, that none can exist without its help and that a society is great and brilliant only so far as it preserves the blood of the noble group that created it. [13]

Servitude, Exploitation, and Abuse

This kind of thinking became a rationale for Spanish decimation of native peoples in Cuba, Hispaniola, Mexico, and other lands. Between 1495 and 1515, the Spanish worked to death or simply murdered outright 80 percent of Hispaniola's original 250,000 inhabitants. By 1550 only 500 of the natives were left. And by 1650 all had been exterminated. White feelings of superiority were also behind Portuguese mistreat-

ment of the natives of Brazil; British abuses of the black Aborigines in Australia; and the enslavement of black Africans by the Portuguese, French, British, and others. Usually the black slaves were shipped out of Africa to other parts of the world.

However, slavery existed within Europe's African colonies as well. For example, in the Cape Colony, located in the continent's southernmost sector, Dutch and later British settlers owned, exploited, and often abused slaves. Britain abolished slavery in all of its colonies in 1834, but blacks in the Cape Colony were still seen and treated as inferiors. Racial tensions continued well into the twentieth century, after the colony had become the nation of South Africa, with the institution of the policy of apartheid, which ordered that the white and black races be kept as separate as possible.

Nonwhites were not the only people in the colonies who were exploited and abused by the authorities. Some whites came to the colonies as indentured servants. An indentured servant was a person who belonged to and did work for someone else for a specified period of time. In theory, this temporary servitude was intended to pay off a debt owed to the master. At first, the most common debt incurred was the master's payment of the servant's ship passage from the mother country to the colony. Scholar Lauren A. Kattner describes the example of white Germans and French who went as indentured servants to Britain's and France's North American colonies: "Adults worked three to six years [to pay off the debt they owed for their passage to America]. Children and youths worked

Converting the Natives to Christianity

One of the methods used by European colonizers to maintain control of native peoples was to attempt to convert these peoples to Christianity. In doing so, the Christian missionaries usually dismissed native beliefs as mere superstition and treated the natives in a patronizing manner. Typical were these words (quoted in Wilcomb E. Washburn's The Indian and the White Man) spoken to the chief of the Seneca tribe (in what is now northern New York State) by a missionary from Britain's Massachusetts colony:

There is but one religion, and but one way to serve God, and if you do not embrace the right way, you cannot be happy hereafter. You have never worshipped the Great Spirit in a manner acceptable to him; but have, all your lives, been in great errors and darkness. To endeavor to remove these errors, and open your eyes, so that you might see clearly, is my business with you.

A European missionary attempts to convert Native Americans to Christianity in Pennsylvania in the 1760s.

until age twenty-one. In some cases, children paid the passage for elderly relatives by working extra years."[14] This system was widely abused. Some indentured servants served their time and gained their freedom. But many others were cheated by unscrupulous masters and fell into what amounted to permanent slavery.

Fierce Competition

Thus, displacing or enslaving native peoples and/or shipping in slaves or indentured servants were among the principal methods that colonies used both to maintain local control and to turn a profit. And most of Europe's overseas colonies did prove to be financially successful. Indeed, in some cases they were phenomenally so. By 1780 St. Domingue alone accounted for 40 percent of France's foreign trade and represented a major component of the country's economy.

With the potential for such wealth from colonial possessions, it is not surprising that competition for colonies among the great powers was fierce. Wars over colonies and the trade routes that linked them were inevitable. These powers "believed that the improvement of one nation's position could only be achieved at the expense of another," Syracuse University scholar Alan K. Smith points out, so "Europeans fought each other for commercial supremacy in the four corners of the globe."[15] Some of the biggest of these wars took place during the 1700s. But these were not the only struggles that shook that century. To the surprise of the great powers, the inhabitants of some of their most valuable colonies suddenly decided that they wanted to be free.

Chapter Three

Early Resistance to Colonialism

By the mid-1700s Europe's numerous overseas colonies in North and South America, the Far East, and elsewhere were thriving. The mother countries reaped handsome profits from the raw materials and trade these distant outposts provided. In the process the Europeans also gained power and prestige. And they frequently tried to gain the upper hand over one another, particularly by fighting over their colonial possessions.

These skirmishes and small-scale wars culminated in a larger conflict—the Seven Years' War, fought between Britain and France, and their respective allies, from 1756 until 1763. The war was declared over disputes within Europe itself. But much of the fighting took place in Europe's colonies around the world and was motivated by the desire of the great powers to expand their overseas empires. The North American theater of the war, in which the French and British each allied themselves with various Native American tribes, became known as the French and Indian Wars.

Britain won the war and gained much colonial territory around the globe as a result, most notably southern Canada and much of the Ohio Valley. What the British did not realize at the time was that they would soon lose a large and valuable portion of their colonial territory—namely, their American colonies. The great powers were used to losing colonies to one another in their incessant competition for world dominance. But they had not yet experienced, nor had they seriously anticipated, such losses through colonial rebellions. The American Revolution, which began in 1775, proved to be only the first of several major colonial revolts that shook the world in the late 1700s and early 1800s. England, Spain, and France were the biggest losers. The colonies they lost in North and South America became independent nations, thereby redrawing the map of the Western Hemisphere.

No Happiness Without Freedom

The attitude of many American colonists toward the Stamp Act and other taxes imposed by the British was summed up in the twelve so-called Farmer's Letters *written by Philadelphia lawyer John Dickinson. In the twelfth letter (quoted here from Morison's* Sources and Documents Illustrating the American Revolution*), he states:*

L et these truths be indelibly impressed on our minds—that we cannot be happy without being free—that we cannot be free without being secure in our property—that we cannot be secure in our property if without our consent others may . . . take it away—that taxes imposed on us by Parliament do thus take it away—that duties raised for the sole purpose of raising money are taxes—that attempts to lay such duties should be instantly and firmly opposed—that this opposition can never be effectual unless it is the united effort of these provinces.

American farmer and patriot John Dickinson gave voice to colonial desires for independence.

But though the outcomes of these successful rebellions were similar, their causes and individual experiences were different. Settlement colonies rebelled for different reasons than colonies of exploitation, for example. In settlement colonies, such as Britain's and Spain's American colonies, populations grew larger over time and the colonists felt more and more distant and distinct from the mother countries. Inevitably, the colonists increasingly desired to rule themselves. In contrast, colonies of exploitation, such as France's St. Domingue, lacked large populations of European descent. In these colonies the whites were greatly outnumbered by native peoples and slaves, who eventually asserted themselves by launching rebellions.

An examination of four of the colonial rebellions of this period reveals the different kinds of colonial resistance and the range of the outcomes. These four uprisings resulted in the formation of the United States, Venezuela, Mexico, and Haiti. They were important not only for their individual success and influence at the time but also for providing models that inspired later colonial rebellions in other regions.

The Birth of the United States

In this respect, the American Revolution was by far the most influential of the colonial insurrections. As John W. Cell remarks:

> The American Revolution left a powerful legacy of ideas—particularly the Declaration of Independence and its principle of the equality of all people. These ideas influenced other colonial resistance movements, particularly in Latin America. In many ways the revolt of the Spanish American colonies in the 1810s and 1820s was based on the principles of the American Revolution. [16]

No matter how much other peoples were inspired by the American example, however, the circumstances leading to the rebellion were largely unique to the American colonies. Some of the grievances that led to armed resistance developed from the turbulent wake of the French and Indian Wars. Following their 1763 victory over France, the British needed money to pay for the upkeep of the troops guarding the conquered territories. British leaders hoped to shift the burden away from taxpayers in Britain by taxing the American colonists instead. The American Revenue Act of 1764 placed taxes on sugar and luxury products entering the American colonies. Then came the Stamp Act in 1765. It taxed paper products of all kinds, from newspaper stock to college diplomas and playing cards.

Colonial reactions to the Stamp Act were loud and angry. In Virginia's assembly, the House of Burgesses, legislator Patrick Henry declared that anyone who supported such unfair taxes should be

Patrick Henry delivers one of his fiery speeches protesting British abuses of the colonies.

labeled an enemy of the colony. Thanks to similar protests in the other American colonies, Parliament relented and repealed the Stamp Act in March 1766.

However, Britain still needed money to pay for the upkeep of its troops. So in 1767 Parliament imposed a series of import duties (taxes) on goods Britain shipped to the colonies, including lead, glass, paint, paper, and tea. In reaction, many American merchants boycotted these goods. Also, colonial leaders urged people to make glass, paint, and some other products locally, to wear American-made clothes, and to drink only tea that had been grown in America.

This strategy worked. The British lost so much money that Parliament had to repeal the duties. The one exception was the duty on imported tea. This led to more trouble when, in December 1773, a gang of local Bostonians disguised themselves as Indians and dumped 342 chests of tea into the ocean.

Now it was the turn of the British to be outraged. They saw the so-called Boston Tea Party as a disgraceful act of vandalism and demanded that Britain's leaders retaliate. In response, between March and June 1774, Parliament passed the Coercive Acts (called the Intolerable Acts in the colonies). They closed the port of Boston,

British regulars and colonial militiamen clash in Lexington in 1775. This proved to be the first battle of the American Revolution.

limited the authority of local government, and began housing British troops in colonial homes.

Making an example of Boston turned out to be a mistake. All of the American colonies united in opposition to what they saw as British abuses. In May 1774 more than eighty prominent Virginians, among them Patrick Henry, George Washington, and Thomas Jefferson, issued a resolution that stated, "An attack made on one of our sister colonies, to compel submission to arbitrary taxes, is an attack made on all British America, and threatens ruin to the rights of all, unless the united wisdom of the whole be applied."[17]

Colonial leaders subsequently called for the king and Parliament to act reasonably, cancel the Intolerable Acts, and refrain from further attempts to tax the colonies. But such appeals were in vain. Tensions continued to escalate until bloody battles erupted between colonial militiamen and British soldiers in Lexington and Concord in Massachusetts in 1775. This violence proved to be the point of no return. In July of the following year representatives from the colonies met in Philadelphia and declared their independence.

The Great Liberator

The birth of the United States in 1776 and its military victory over Britain seven years later were events that truly shook the world. The British had not only lost a huge source of revenue, they had also embarrassed themselves by their inability to defeat the Americans, whose numbers and military strength had been far less than their own. Even more importantly, the defeat of one of the most powerful nations on Earth by its own colonists inspired many who dwelled in other European colonies.

This was especially true in the Spanish colonies that shared the Western Hemisphere with the infant United States. Like Britain's former American colonies, Spanish outposts like Venezuela and New Spain (present-day Mexico) were settlement colonies. Also like the British colonials, over time the Spanish colonials steadily grew apart from their mother country. But the situation in the Spanish colonies was somewhat different. In recent years Spain had lost a great deal of power and prestige and was not nearly as militarily strong as Britain. Also, most of Spain's major American colonies lay a good deal farther from Europe than Britain's American colonies lay from Britain. So it was logistically much more difficult and expensive for the Spanish to maintain, much less put down rebellions in, these faraway lands.

Eventually, a group of colonists in Venezuela, in the northernmost sector of South America, decided to take advantage of Spain's weakness and fight for their independence. They were led by two Venezuelan patriots. One was Simón Bolívar, a well-to-do planter; the other was Francisco de Miranda, a professional soldier who had fought on the American side during the American Revolution. In 1810 Bolívar journeyed to London and urged the British to recognize an independent Venezuela. The arguments he used were similar to those he voiced in a later speech, in which he echoed the feelings

Bolívar Offers His Opponents Amnesty

In his Proclamation to the People of Venezuela, *issued in June 1813, Simón Bolívar eloquently reached out to those colonists who were siding with Spain, asking them to join the revolution and warning of the consequences if they did not.*

They are invited to live peacefully among us, if they will abjure [renounce] their crimes, honestly change their ways, and cooperate with us in destroying the intruding Spanish government. . . . Any Spaniard who does not, by every active and effective means, work against tyranny in behalf of this just cause, will be considered an enemy and punished. As a traitor to the nation, he will inevitably be shot by a firing squad. On the other hand, a general and absolute amnesty is granted to those who come over to our army with or without their arms, as well as to those who render aid to the good citizens who are endeavoring to throw off the yoke of tyranny.

Venezuelan patriot Simón Bolívar sparked revolutionary movements in several South American colonies.

of numerous colonists of European descent around the world:

We are not Europeans. We are not Indians. . . . [Instead, we are] Americans by birth and Europeans by law. . . . [Venezuela] should have a republican government. Its principles should be the sovereignty of the people, division of powers, civil liberty . . . and the abolition of monarchy and [aristocratic] privileges. We need equality to [become] a unified nation.[18]

Britain granted the recognition Bolívar sought in 1811. But the Spanish authorities were not so accommodating. They reinforced their troops in South America and defeated Bolívar and Miranda in battle. Undaunted, however, the revolutionaries stubbornly refused to accept defeat. In the years that followed Bolívar staged several bold comebacks, and by June 1821 Venezuela was free of Spanish rule. Not content with this impressive accomplishment, Bolívar went on to help liberate other parts of South America from Spain. These areas eventually became the nations of Peru, Colombia, Ecuador, and Bolivia (named for Bolívar). For these efforts, Bolívar earned the title of "the Great Liberator."

"The Hour of Our Liberty Has Struck"

The South American revolutions against Spain were successful in part because the Spanish were preoccupied with another major colonial rebellion during the same period. Farther north, in Central America, stretched Spain's large and profitable colony of New Spain. Many of the colony's inhabitants had, like their neighbors to the north and south, grown dissatisfied with European rule.

At the root of the discontent in New Spain were grievances based on class, privilege, and a lack of social and economic opportunity for large sectors of the population. The loudest voices of complaint were those of the criolles (or Creoles), people of Spanish descent who had been born in New Spain. They strongly objected to being treated like second-class citizens by the *grachupines*, colonists who had been born in Spain. The *grachupines* held most positions of authority and enjoyed favors from the Spanish king. Hoping to break the power of the *grachupines*, the criolles decided to seek independence from Spain. The criolles were supported by another group of colonists—the mestizos. The offspring of mixed marriages between Spanish colonists and local Indians, the mestizos were mostly poor and treated as inferiors by the ruling class. They hoped that independence would improve their lives.

The first of several uprisings took place in September 1810, when a large group of mestizos marched on the colonial capital, Mexico City. They were led by an educated and politically radical priest named Miguel Hidalgo. In what is now seen as the seminal statement of Mexican liberty, he declared in part:

> The hour of our liberty has struck. And if you recognize its great value, you will help me defend it from the ambitious grasp of the tyrants. . . . [Without] liberty we shall always be at a great distance from true happiness. . . . The cause is holy and God will protect it. . . . Long live, then, the Virgin of Guadalupe! Long live [Spanish] America for which we are going to fight![19]

Unfortunately for the rebels, the *grachupines* easily put down the uprising and killed Hidalgo. However, many Mexicans were inspired to continue the struggle for freedom. In 1814 some better organized rebels led by Hidalgo's pupil, Maria Morelos, gained control of most of southern Mexico. Once more, the ruling class, supported by the Spanish crown, prevailed and quashed the revolt. Yet the spirit of independence could not be stopped. The great turning point came in 1821, when Augustín de Iturbide, a wealthy landowner, persuaded most of the *grachupines* to join the revolution. Seeing that they had

Maria Morelos was one of a series of Mexican patriots who fought Spanish authorities.

no other choice, Spanish leaders granted Mexico independence in August of that year.

The Mexican revolutionaries, who had been inspired to some degree by the American Revolution, proceeded to adopt a constitution similar in some ways to that of the United States. They then turned their attention to the land. The former colony had encompassed a huge expanse—more than 1 million square miles (2.6 million sq. km) in all. The government divided it into nineteen provinces, or states, and four territories. By the late 1820s, therefore, large portions of the North and South American mainlands had been transformed from European colonies into independently ruled nations and states.

Slaves Who Fought for Freedom

The mainlands were not the only portions of the Western Hemisphere in which the European colonial powers suffered major losses. Independence movements grew in some of the island plantation colonies as well. The biggest and most successful of these rebellions occurred in France's St. Domingue.

Unlike the revolutions in the mainland settlement colonies, the one in St. Domingue was essentially a slave rebellion rather than a revolt of free businessmen and workers. Because it was a colony of exploitation, St. Domingue had relatively few white European residents. And the vast majority of them were satisfied to maintain the status quo, in which they continued to reap the financial benefits of supplying France with sugarcane, coffee, and other cash crops.

Slaves Comforted by Traditional Beliefs

A majority of the black slaves who worked and suffered in St. Domingue, or their parents or grandparents, came from the west African region now occupied by Benin. This was the homeland of a group of tribal peoples known as the Yoruba. After their capture, they brought their religion with them to the colony. However, the French, who were Christians, would not allow them to openly practice their traditional rituals. So these rites had to be performed in secret. Over the course of time, the names and roles of some of the spirits they had long worshipped changed to fit the conditions in which they lived. For example, the chief Yoruba spirit, Ogun, associated with hunting and warfare, became Ogoun, to whom the slaves prayed to give them strength to withstand the horrors they had to endure on the French plantations. In this way, their faith gave them at least a small measure of comfort. Eventually, the Haitian version of the Yoruba faith came to be called Vodoun, which outsiders call Voodoo.

Meanwhile, the hundreds of thousands of slaves who performed the menial labor needed to raise these crops lived in the worst poverty and misery imaginable. They worked long hours in the tropical sun, often until they fainted or died from exhaustion. Those who did not work fast enough were brutally whipped. A slave who broke even a minor rule had nails driven through his ears, his sex organs mutilated, or his arm plunged into boiling cane syrup. Some slaves were killed simply to intimidate the others. These atrocities were carried out by a small class of professional torturers and executioners who lived on the island and even had their fees set by law.

Eventually, the slaves started fighting back. Some ran away and lived in secret locations in the mountains. These Maroons, as the French called them, conducted raids on white plantations. In August 1791 a Maroon-led rebellion erupted in the northern part of St. Domingue. Its leader, Boukman Dutty, declared:

> The god who created the sun which gives us light, who rouses the waves and rules the storm . . . watches us. He sees all that the white man does. The god of the white man inspires him with crime, but our god calls upon us to do good works. Our god . . . will direct our arms and aid us. . . . Listen to the voice of liberty, which speaks in the hearts of us all. [20]

The rebellion soon engulfed the entire colony. Other black leaders rose from among the slaves, the most skilled and famous being Toussaint-Louverture. These men guided the slaves in several military

Toussaint Louverture was the most famous of the black revolutionaries who freed St. Domingue from French control.

victories over the French. And St. Domingue became the independent nation of Haiti in 1803.

Shattering a Myth

The Haitians' success, along with successful colonial resistance in other parts of the Americas during that era, had far-reaching consequences for the European powers and the American lands themselves. Spain's colonial losses were permanent, for example. They ultimately reduced the nation from a first-rate to a second-rate power in world affairs. Also, the revolt in Haiti spoiled the plans of France's dictator, Napoléon Bonaparte, who planned to use the colony as a base from which to conquer the Americas.

If nothing else, these successful rebellions shattered the myth of European invincibility. They showed that freedom from the European colonial powers could be achieved through courage and perseverance.

Chapter Four

"The Sun Never Sets": Britain's Empire Expands

The successful rebellions in Britain's, Spain's, and France's American colonies during the late 1700s and early 1800s marked the end of a major phase of European colonialism and the beginning of another. The new phase, lasting roughly from 1815 to 1880, was dominated almost entirely by the British. French, Dutch, Spanish, and other European colonial activity in this period was minimal at best.

The reasons for Britain's lack of competition in this era varied. Spain, of course, had suffered the loss of most of its American colonies and was no longer a major world power. The Dutch, too, had significantly declined in power in recent years. Meanwhile, the French were exhausted from the rigors of the period from 1789 to 1815, during which they had endured the French Revolution and its aftermath—the bloody Napoleonic Wars. Thus, as Louis L. Snyder sums it up, "After the defeat of Napoleon [in 1815] there remained but one strong colonial empire of any consequence—the British."[21]

Britain expanded its influence across much of the globe in the nineteenth century without establishing many formal new colonies. More often, it exploited the markets and influenced the affairs of existing nations and colonies while imposing little or no direct rule on them. These regions then became heavily dependent economically on trade with Britain and its empire. About this brand of imperialism, which modern historians often call free-trade imperialism, scholar Robert Y. Eng writes:

> The British pioneered in informal imperialism, or the acquisition of commercial privileges, including access to [foreign] markets for their industrial goods and sources of raw materials and agricultural goods . . . as opposed to formal imperialism, or the acquisition of colonies that would

incur administrative costs of governing.[22]

Thus, trade and economic relationships were the backbone of Britain's expanding empire. To create and maintain these relationships, the British largely employed negotiation, including treaties that were often weighted heavily in favor of Britain. But they also possessed considerable firepower to fall back on when negotiation failed. Sometimes their navy, the largest in the world, and their highly organized, well-trained army enforced their will on local rulers and populations who presented obstacles to Britain's policies. Through trade, negotiation, and occasional armed force, therefore, the British involved themselves in India, China, Singapore, Egypt, South Africa, Australia, and many other places. It was in this period that someone coined the now famous and quite accurate phrase "the sun never sets on the British Empire."

"The White Man's Burden"

Politicians, scholars, and others have long argued over whether British imperialism was good for the lands and peoples it affected. Some have called it bad, saying that Britain frequently exploited less-developed regions at the expense of the natives. The natives almost always had fewer civil rights and privileges than the British colonizers, traders, and soldiers. And British merchants and planters grew rich thanks to the cheap labor of the natives, most of whom lived in poverty. The other side of the argument is that Britain brought industry, roads, ports, and

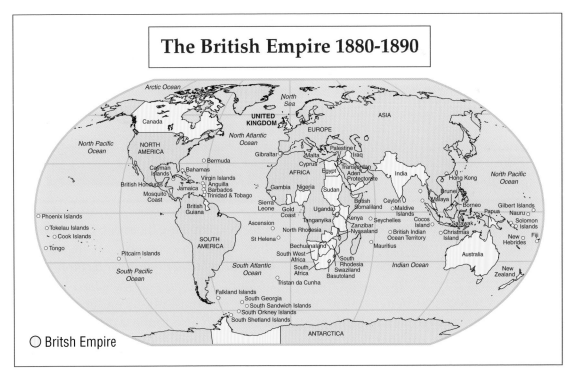

The British Empire 1880-1890

○ British Empire

Kipling Defends Imperialism

Rudyard Kipling, whose poem "The White Man's Burden" concisely captured the attitude of the colonial powers during the nineteenth century, was born in Bombay, India, in December 1865. Eventually he became a newspaper reporter and editor in Lahore, in present-day Pakistan. In addition to his newspaper work, Kipling wrote short stories and poetry, much of which became world famous and influential. His 1888 short story "The Man Who Would Be King" was widely popular and later, in 1975, it was made into a major motion picture starring Sean Connery, Michael Caine, and Christopher Plummer, who played Kipling. The story, like "The White Man's Burden," defends imperialism and reflects Kipling's steadfast belief that it was Britain's unenviable duty to civilize the "backward" natives.

British journalist Rudyard Kipling saw Britain as a civilizing influence.

increased prosperity to many areas that had lacked these advantages.

What is undeniable is that the nineteenth-century British themselves viewed their colonial endeavors as beneficial to all involved. There was a sense among British thinkers and politicians that they were doing foreign peoples a favor either by directly colonizing them or by dominating them through economic means. In this view, British imperialism and colonization brought progress and increased levels of prosperity not only to underdeveloped regions but also to the world as a whole. The noted English economist John Stuart Mill (1806–1873) ably summed up this attitude in his 1848 essay "On Colonies and Colonization." "To appreciate the benefits of colonization," he states,

it should be considered in its relation, not to a single country, but to the collective economical interests of the human race. . . . The exportation of laborers and capital from old to new countries, from a place where their productive power is less, to a place where it is greater, [significantly] increases . . . [the overall output] of the labor and capital of the world. It adds to the joint wealth of the old and the new country. . . . There needs be no hesitation in affirming that colonization, in the present state of the

world, is the best affair of business in which . . . an old and wealthy country can engage.[23]

Many British went so far as to say that it was the responsibility, sometimes a regrettable one, of the British to help "civilize" the world. According to this view, Britain and other strong, white-dominated nations had the best culture, religion, and ideas. And it was their duty to introduce those qualities to less-developed, non-white peoples for their own good, by force if necessary. This so-called duty eventually came to be known as "the white man's burden." The term derived from the title of a widely influential poem by Rudyard Kipling, a British writer born in colonial

An Indian servant waits on a British soldier in nineteenth-century India. The British saw it as their mission to "civilize" non-whites.

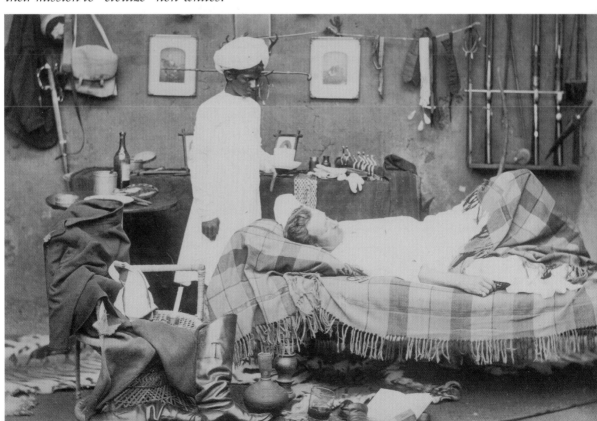

India in 1865. His words neatly summarized the arrogant attitude of nineteenth-century British imperialists as well as later European and American imperialists. The poem reads in part:

Take up the White Man's burden—
Ye dare not stoop to less—
Nor call too loud on Freedom
To cloak your weariness;
By all ye cry or whisper,
By all ye leave or do,
The silent, sullen peoples
Shall weigh your gods and you.[24]

The Coming of the Raj

In writing these words, Kipling was profoundly influenced by his experiences growing up in British colonial India. Before the nineteenth century, the North American colonies had been the most important of Britain's overseas possessions. But following the loss of these colonies as a result of the American Revolution, the British switched the main focus of their colonial endeavors to India.

There, the British East India Company had established lucrative trading posts during the 1600s and early 1700s. By the mid-1700s, the local Mughal Empire had become fragmented into many smaller, weaker regional states. The East India Company exploited the situation by forcefully subduing some of these states while making strategic alliances with others. Some British soldiers were used in these operations. But most of the fighting was done by sepoys, Indian troops trained by and loyal to the British.

By the early nineteenth century, therefore, some parts of India were under direct British control. And most others either had treaties with the British or were at least indirectly affected by British policies in the region. On behalf of the British government, but also working for its own interests, the East India Company stepped up its aggressive expansionist policies in the first half of the century.

The company ran into trouble, however, when it blatantly annexed the state of Oudh in north-central India in 1856. This was the last substantial vestige of the Mughal Empire, and company officials made it clear that that realm would soon cease to exist. This heavy-handed approach, combined with mounting grievances over British interference in local Indian culture, ignited a large-scale mutiny among the sepoys in northern India. The rebels fought well and bravely. However, British troops, supported by loyal sepoys, managed to put down the insurrection.

In the wake of the rebellion, the British changed their approach to dealing with India. The government in London abolished the East India Company and instituted direct British rule over those Indian regions the company had controlled. Subsequent British rule in India came to be known as the British Raj. Because the mutiny had instilled fear in the local whites, their already considerable prejudice against native Indians increased during the Raj's early decades. And the lives of people in the two groups became increasingly separate, as whites largely kept to their own guarded communities and private social clubs.

The Causes of the Indian Rebellion

In this excerpt from her book on imperialism, Rutgers University scholar Bonnie G. Smith elaborates on the accumulated British abuses that touched off the great Indian uprising of 1857.

Over a period of years the British East India Company had ridden roughshod over a number of Indian customs. . . . The company had attacked the caste system that classified Indians into strictly regulated groups, while missionaries had encouraged Indians' conversion to Christianity. The introduction of a new rifle into the Indian army also became offensive, because soldiers had to bite the end off cartridges that had been greased with a mixture of beef and pork fat. The sepoys rebelled because beef and pork were meats forbidden to Hindus and Muslims respectively. Although this blatant disregard for both sets of religious laws infuriated Indian soldiers, the mutiny sparked the smoldering resentments of princes and members of the middle and upper classes, who were becoming increasingly outraged at the East India Company's . . . attacks on important social customs.

The leaders of the sepoy rebellion are executed by strapping them to cannons and opening fire.

One result of British feelings of superiority was the colonial government's neglect of the many economic and social problems faced by the locals, most of whom were dirt poor. "Critics accused the British of failing to solve the problems of the Indian caste system, infanticide, illiteracy, poverty, famine, and disease," Snyder points out. "In defense, the British pointed to their construction of roads and railways, the establishment of schools and universities, and improvements in [law] and the administration of justice."[25] This difference of opinion over the impact of British domination of India was destined to endure into the next century, when the Indians finally gained their independence.

The Eastern Route and Egypt

In the meantime, a large portion of nineteenth-century Britain's global trade and colonial policies were either directly or indirectly connected to its exploitation of India. For example, British ships traveling to and from India at first used the route that passes by the Cape of Good Hope, located at Africa's southern tip. Partly to ensure that this route would remain secure, in the 1790s Britain began colonizing the area around Cape Town. For added control of the region, the British later established a colony at Natal, on Africa's southeastern coast.

Still, this route to India was long and time-consuming, and the British hoped to

Constructed by the French and Egyptians in the 1860s, the Suez Canal provided Europeans with a maritime shortcut to the Far East.

find a shorter one. They accomplished this goal by taking control of the Suez Canal, linking the Mediterranean and Red seas, in the 1870s. The canal had been constructed in the 1860s by a joint French and Egyptian venture. Seeing that control of Egypt was necessary for the security of the canal, the British searched for an excuse to intervene in that country. An opportunity came in 1882, when the Egyptian government, which was on the verge of bankruptcy, faced a rebellion within its own army ranks. Saying that outside intervention was necessary to restore both order and the local economy, the British seized control of Egypt in 1882.

Egypt became a textbook case of British free-trade imperialism. It was not a colony in the traditional sense but rather more of a protectorate. The country had its own native leaders. But they were expected to follow the advice of British political and economic advisers. In spite of the fact that they lacked complete political autonomy, the Egyptians did benefit in some ways from the British presence. To protect its financial and political investments in Egypt, Britain improved the local economy, built schools, and retrained the Egyptian army according to British methods and standards, as had been done with the sepoys in India.

In the view of many Egyptians, however, these positive aspects of British occupation were often overshadowed by less-constructive ones. British advisers, officials, merchants, and soldiers maintained their usual air of superiority over the nonwhite natives, which led to discrimination and bad feelings. In an unapologetic expression

An 1893 illustration from a European journal captured the British attitude toward native Egyptians.

of racism and Western arrogance, Evelyn Baring, the leading British official in Egypt, stated:

[Lack] of accuracy which easily degenerates into untruthfulness, is, in fact, the main characteristic of the [Middle Eastern or Asian] mind. The European is a close reasoner. His statements of fact are devoid of ambiguity. . . . His trained intelligence works like a [machine]. The mind of the Oriental, on the other hand . . . is eminently wanting in symmetry. His reasoning is of the most slipshod description. . . . Endeavor to [get] a plain statement of facts from an ordinary Egyptian. . . . He will probably contradict himself half a dozen times before he has finished his story.[26]

China and the Opium Wars

Maintaining control of Egypt and the route through the Suez Canal was not the only way the British protected their interests in India. To the greatest extent they could, they also sought to control the trade routes and regions surrounding India. On the one hand, this would reduce or eliminate the presence of European competitors and thereby keep India's borders and markets safely in Britain's fold. On the other, the British would have new markets to exploit in eastern Asia. Of these markets, early nineteenth-century British imperialists realized, China was potentially one of the most valuable.

One reason that China had not been economically exploited by outsiders before that century was that foreign traders were long unable to find a commodity that would sell well there. Finally, in the early 1800s, they found success with opium, a drug derived from the poppy plant. The British began growing poppies in India, where the opium was extracted and shipped to the southern Chinese port of Canton. In this way, British traders rapidly made fortunes selling the drug to the Chinese, whose society suffered greatly as a result. In an 1838 tract titled "The Evil of Opium," a Chinese official wrote:

At the beginning, opium smoking was confined to the fops [idle young men] of wealthy families. . . . Later, people of all social strata—from government officials . . . to craftsmen, merchants . . . servants, and even women [and] Buddhist monks—took up the habit. . . . Even in . . . the nation's capital and its surrounding areas, some of the inhabitants have also been contaminated by this dreadful poison.[27]

Worried Chinese leaders took steps to suppress the opium trade in 1838, and the British immediately saw this as an opportunity to gain more control over China. The following year Britain sent troops to that country and launched what became known as the First Opium War. The conflict ended in 1842 with the British the decisive victors. They forced Chinese leaders to sign the Treaty of Nanking. Under its provisions, the port of Hong Kong became a British colony and China had to open four additional ports to British commerce. Later, Britain provoked another conflict with China—the Second Opium War (1865–1860)—which resulted in still more ports opening to foreigners as well as complete freedom of movement for European missionaries in China. The British also gained the legal right to sell opium in China, and some of the resulting profits helped to pay for their costly administration of India.

Singapore and the Pacific Region

Nineteenth-century Britain's efforts to control Eastern markets extended well beyond

India and China. Along the route between these lands, at the tip of the Malay Peninsula, lay the tiny island of Singapore. England's Sir Thomas Stamford Raffles landed there in 1818 and set up a trading post. Five years later the British East India Company took control of the colony. Singapore became not only a strategic resupply depot for ships traveling between India and China but also a rich exporter of rubber, tin, and other raw materials extracted from southern Asia.

Meanwhile, in the Pacific region the British established settlement colonies in Australia and New Zealand. The settlement in southeastern Australia, which became New South Wales, began as a penal colony in 1788. Between that date and 1856, some 160,000 prisoners from across the British Empire were deposited in the region. Most were not held in prisons but rather worked as servants and laborers for well-to-do free colonists. Eventually, as more and more free settlers arrived, the convicts became integrated into the general population.

Whether they were prisoners or free persons, the vast majority of Australian

British warships bombard the Chinese city of Canton in 1841, during the First Opium War. Upon defeat, china was forced to open its ports to the British.

Raffles Establishes Singapore

Singapore, long one of Britain's most successful colonies, was established by Sir Thomas Stamford Raffles. Born in 1781 in another British colony, Jamaica, Raffles began working for the British East India Company in London while still a teenager. He became a high official in the Indonesian colony of Java in 1811 and not long afterward was promoted to the post of governor of Sumatra. In 1818 Raffles founded a trading post on a small island at the southern tip of the Malay Peninsula. This trading post grew into the colony of Singapore. Among Raffles's accomplishments in Singapore was a plan—supervised by the colony's engineer, Philip Jackson—to lay out the central town in an efficient grid pattern. Raffles left Singapore in 1823, never to return. He had no way of knowing that his creation would later become one of the world's largest and busiest ports.

Thomas Stamford Raffles established the colony of Singapore on the Malay Peninsula in 1818.

colonists were white. And they looked down on and oppressed the black Aborigines who made up the native population. Once more, racism and discrimination made their mark, as they had in India, Egypt, China, and other areas colonized or exploited by Britain in the 1800s. The British undoubtedly accomplished much of a constructive nature across the globe in this period. But in the long run, many positive achievements were overshadowed by the poor treatment of native peoples. The resentments of these peoples would linger into the next century and help to reshape the world in ways that would surely have shocked and appalled most of the nineteenth-century imperialists.

Chapter Five

The New Imperialism and Scramble for Africa

During much of the nineteenth century Britain enjoyed a near monopoly on imperial expansion and exploitation of lands and peoples across the globe. But this lopsided British dominance of the colonial pie was not destined to endure. By the 1870s and 1880s, other nations began to seek their own pieces of that pie. This ignited a new burst of colonialism—the largest the world had yet witnessed—lasting from about 1880 to the start of World War I in 1914. Later observers came to call it the New Imperialism. Although colonial acquisitions occurred all over the world, the two main spheres of activity in this period were Africa and the Pacific region. All told, by 1914 the major colonial powers had added a whopping 20 percent of Earth's total land area to their domains.

The main participants in this massive new round of colonial activity consisted of a mix of old and new players. Britain and France loomed large, and Spain and Portugal attempted to stay in the game, hoping to recover from their major colonial losses in prior eras. Other important European players included Belgium and newcomers Germany and Italy, which had only recently become unified nations. Meanwhile, far beyond Europe's borders, the United States and Japan had begun to emerge as industrial powers. They saw a need to compete with Europe for pieces of the globe or else be left in the dust in the ongoing struggle for power and influence.

The motives behind this struggle varied. But as in earlier stages of colonialism, they mostly involved attempts to assert political dominance and reap the largest economic advantages possible. First, France, Germany, the United States, and most of the others sought to break Britain's stranglehold on international markets. All agreed that the best way to do this was to seize and exploit their own colonial possessions. There was also an urgent demand for raw materials, especially rubber, copper, tin,

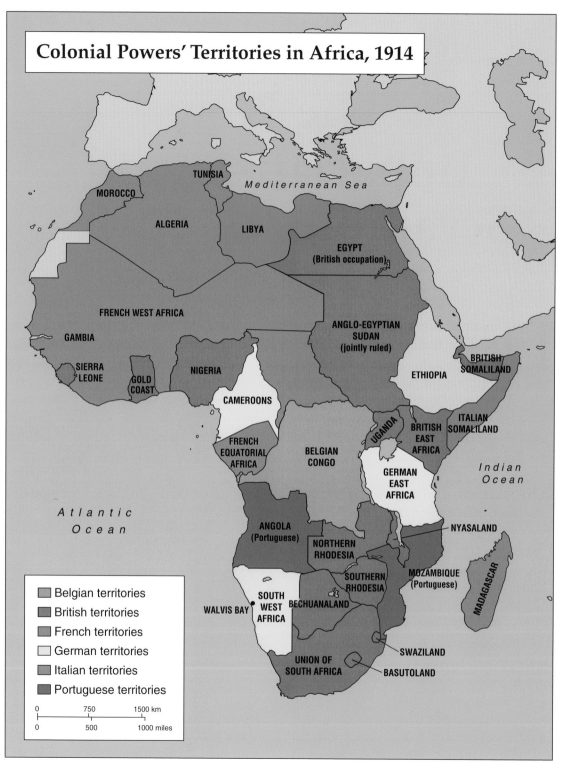

Colonial Powers' Territories in Africa, 1914

TUNISIA

MOROCCO

ALGERIA

LIBYA

Mediterranean Sea

EGYPT
(British occupation)

FRENCH WEST AFRICA

ANGLO-EGYPTIAN
SUDAN
(jointly ruled)

GAMBIA

SIERRA
LEONE

GOLD
COAST

NIGERIA

ETHIOPIA

BRITISH
SOMALILAND

CAMEROONS

UGANDA

BRITISH
EAST
AFRICA

ITALIAN
SOMALILAND

FRENCH
EQUATORIAL
AFRICA

BELGIAN
CONGO

GERMAN
EAST
AFRICA

*Indian
Ocean*

*Atlantic
Ocean*

ANGOLA
(Portuguese)

NORTHERN
RHODESIA

NYASALAND

MOZAMBIQUE
(Portuguese)

MADAGASCAR

SOUTHERN
RHODESIA

WALVIS BAY

SOUTH
WEST
AFRICA

BECHUANALAND

SWAZILAND

UNION OF
SOUTH AFRICA

BASUTOLAND

Belgian territories

British territories

French territories

German territories

Italian territories

Portuguese territories

0   750   1500 km

0   500   1000 miles

cotton, coal, and precious metals. Naturally, these and other materials could be extracted and processed more economically by using cheap labor. And dependent colonial populations were a ready source of underpaid workers.

In addition, recent advances in technology had made exploitation of distant, undeveloped lands more logistically and economically viable. Railways and steam-powered ships could ferry goods and people in and out of remote areas in record time. The telegraph allowed settlers and companies to communicate and coordinate activities more efficiently. And new medicines made catching malaria and other tropical diseases less of an obstacle to colonization.

Another potential obstacle to colonization that had to be dealt with was native resistance. As in past rounds of colonialism, the great powers often tried to pacify the locals by making promises to and treaties with them, both of which were usually broken in time. Just as often, though, the colonizers resorted to violence to control native populations. All the while, they justified everything by adopting the "white-man's-burden" attitude, arguing that they were acting for the natives own good. As John W. Cell points out:

Imperial nations adopted the attitude that they should control these areas in order to protect what they viewed as weak peoples. In general, the citizens of the more powerful nations supported this view, especially because, with the exception of Japan's control of Korea, the power holders were white and their subjects were people of color.[28]

The Partition of Africa

Nowhere did the great powers use the pretext of humanitarian aims to justify naked conquest more blatantly and cruelly than in Africa. Describing an ongoing Belgian venture into central Africa, an article published in London's *Daily Telegraph* in 1884 stated that the colonizer "has knit adventurers, traders, and missionaries of many races into one band of men . . . to carry into the interior of Africa new ideas of law, order, humanity, and protection of the natives."[29]

In fact, such rosy claims and predictions could not have been further from the truth. In what later became known as the scramble for Africa, the world's most powerful nations descended on the continent in what amounted to nothing less then an international feeding frenzy. They were drawn by the promise of seemingly unlimited natural resources. These potential riches had only recently been revealed by white explorers, most notably Scotsman David Livingstone and a Welsh-born American, Henry M. Stanley. A January 1876 article in the *Times* of London summed up what seemed to be waiting in Africa for those Europeans and others willing to invest in colonizing it:

The interior is mostly a magnificent and healthy country of unspeakable richness. . . . Coal [and] other minerals such as gold, copper, iron, and silver, are abundant and I am confident

"An Attila in Modern Dress"

L eopold II, who ruled one of the largest of the European colonies in Africa in the late nineteenth century, was born in Brussels in 1835 and ascended Belgium's throne in 1865. He strongly believed that acquiring overseas colonies would make Belgium one of the greatest countries in the world. When neither the Belgian government nor Belgian people showed any interest in such ventures, the king decided to create an empire and run it on his own. After negotiating with other European leaders for more than a decade, in 1885 he managed to gain control of a large parcel of land in central Africa, which became known as the Congo Free State. The colony was a staggering seventy-six times larger than Belgium. Because Leopold administered the colony so brutally, the Belgian parliament took it away from him in 1908. The king, whom one British historian called an "Attila in modern dress" in reference to the barbarian Attila the Hun, died a year later, a wealthy but hated man.

Leopold II, king of Belgium, led the European rush to exploit the African continent.

that with a wise and liberal . . . expenditure of capital, of the greatest systems of inland navigation in the world [Africa's numerous large rivers] might be utilized, and . . . [in a short time] began to repay an enterprising capitalist that might take the matter in hand. [30]

It rapidly became clear that many Europeans and others were gearing up to exploit the so-called dark continent. These nations recognized that one result of such intense competition might be wars among themselves. Because such conflicts would only impede the profitable colonial enterprises of all, they decided to get together and create guidelines for partitioning, or dividing up, Africa. To this end, the great powers met in Berlin in 1884–1885. They agreed on a concept called effective occupation. Essentially it meant that, in order to claim ownership of an African territory, a country would be required to demonstrate physical control of it through the use of soldiers and settlers, treaties with the natives, and so forth. The country would also have to formally notify the other great powers of its new acquisition. In addition, all the nations attending the Berlin Conference would enjoy free trade and shipping rights throughout most of Africa.

With a few exceptions, these rules set down in Berlin did help avert bloody wars among the great powers. But they addressed only the interests of the colonizers and did little or nothing to safeguard native Africans from abuse. In fact, wholesale abuses were almost guaranteed by the doctrine of effective occupation adopted at the conference. The colonizers regularly tricked the natives into giving up their lands by enticing them to sign treaties with deceptive or vague wording. They also resorted to employing troops to force the natives into submission, and millions of Africans were murdered or intimidated. In the words of English historian Thomas Pakenham, "Europe had imposed its will on Africa at the point of a gun. It was a lesson that would be remembered, fifty years later, when Africa came to win its independence." [31]

In 1900, at the height of Leopold's exploitation of the Congo, a team of Belgian industrialists searches for gold in a local river.

Using such methods, the Europeans laid claim to and partitioned African lands with astonishing swiftness. In 1875 the only significant European colonies on the continent had been Algeria (belonging to France), the Cape Colony (Britain), and Angola (Portugal). By 1914, in contrast, over half of Africa was in colonial hands. Britain controlled about 30 percent; France, 15 percent; Germany, 9 percent; Belgium, 7 percent; and Italy, 1 percent.

Tragedy in the Congo

The manner in which Belgium formed and operated the so-called Congo Free State is vividly illustrative of colonialism in Africa in general. It clearly exposes both the unscrupulous methods of the colonizers and the tragic consequences for the natives.

Well before the advent of the Berlin Conference, Belgium's King Leopold II hoped to expand the colonial holdings of his tiny nation. Yet his aspirations were also selfish, as he dreamed of ruling and exploiting the riches of his own personal kingdom in Africa. To this end, in 1876 he formed the International African Association. A private organization, its supposed goal was to develop an African region in an honest and humanitarian manner. Leopold also lobbied hard behind the scenes with the leaders of many of the great powers to gain support for his venture. Thus, when the Berlin Conference convened, granting Leopold his kingdom became a priority of all involved. "Such a concept was attractive to Britain and Germany," writes noted scholar of African history Robert W. July,

as a check to French ambitions in the area. And all sides were cordial toward a scheme that blocked Portugal [from gaining a foothold in central Africa]. France was finally [convinced to go along] when she was assured the right to [take over Leopold's colony] in the event he was unable to maintain the costs of administration. [32]

In 1885, only a few months after the conference, Leopold was the proud owner of a private domain in the heart of Africa. It covered an immense expanse of some 905,000 square miles (2.3 million sq. km) and contained about 30 million inhabitants, the vast majority of whom had never heard of Leopold, nor even of Belgium. The name of the place—the Congo Free State—was deceptive since it was anything but free for the natives who lived there. Leopold immediately put large numbers of them to work producing cash crops, especially large vines that contained a form of liquid latex rubber.

To make sure the workers met Leopold's demanding quotas and dared not complain about the fact that they were not paid for their labors, he instituted a reign of terror. His white officials commanded the Force Publique (FP), an army of thugs who mutilated and murdered the populace at will. People routinely suffered beatings, rapes, and the severing of their hands, for which members of the FP received bonuses. Modern estimates for the number of Congolese who died in the approximately two decades of Leopold's rule of the area range from 5 to 20 million.

Eventually, Leopold's strenuous efforts to hide what was going on in the Congo

Leopold's Atrocities Are Revealed

This tract (quoted in Ludwig Bauer's Leopold the Unloved*) is from the report filed by one of the European commissions that investigated the terrible abuses perpetrated by Belgium's King Leopold II in the Congo Free State.*

Within the territories of the Abir [tribe], the chief . . . was murdered, his wife and children being eaten by the cannibal guards. The houses of the natives were decorated with the intestines, the liver, and the heart of the murdered. . . . Children have their brains dashed out. Murders [continue] without ceasing. The bodies of the slain are eaten. Soldiers are flogged by the [Belgian] agents' orders if they have been slack in the work of murder. Women [are] mutilated because they are true to their husbands. The commission spends many hours, many days, listening to such reports. . . . Behind each who complains stand hundreds who do not dare to speak.

Native workers beat masses of raw rubber to remove plant fibers. Millions of these workers were killed by Leopold's men.

failed. Investigative journalists from Britain and elsewhere documented the atrocities and called attention to them in the world press. Most of the nations that had helped Leopold acquire the Congo in Berlin now condemned his actions and demanded that the abuses end. Under much pressure, in 1908 the Belgian parliament relieved Leopold of his personal ownership of the Congo Free State, which became the state-run Belgian Congo. However, Leopold was never punished and got to keep the enormous fortune he had amassed at a terrible cost in human misery.

The United States: Manifest Destiny and Beyond

Among the fourteen nations that had attended the Berlin Conference was the United States. And some of the most vocal critics of Leopold's abuses in Africa were American politicians, journalists, and writers. Prominent among the latter was Mark Twain (Samuel Clemens), who composed a biting satire that ridiculed Leopold—"King Leopold's Soliloquy."

In this same period, Twain, industrialist Andrew Carnegie, and other like-minded Americans were also deeply concerned with what they viewed as their own nation's colonial ambitions. They came to call themselves the American anti-imperialists. In their opinion, the United States had engaged in its own brand of imperialism inside the confines of North America in the nineteenth century, when Britain had dominated global colonial activities. These critics pointed to the doctrine of manifest destiny (a term coined by newspaper editor John O'Sullivan in 1845). It held that God or fate had ordained that Americans should rule all the lands lying between the Atlantic and Pacific oceans. For many Americans, it justified the brutal subjugation of Native American tribes that was already ongoing. Then U.S. leaders provoked Mexico into a bloody conflict, the Mexican-American War (1846–1848), which ended with Mexico ceding huge western territories, including California, to the United States.

American writer Mark Twain helped to found an organization that opposed U.S. imperialism.

By the start of the New Imperialism era (in the 1880s), therefore, the United States had fulfilled its dream of manifest destiny. But to the disgust of the anti-imperialists, this marked only the start of the nation's territorial ambitions. Many prominent Americans agreed with historian Frederick Jackson Turner's "frontier thesis." It held that much of America's underlying strength and vitality had derived from its taming of undeveloped frontiers and that it must now seek new frontiers to exploit. Also influential was historian Alfred T. Mahan's 1890 call for gaining an outpost in the Pacific Ocean to better facilitate trade with Asia, especially China.

Mahan's call was answered only a few years later. In 1893 some of the mostly American-run businesses in the Hawaiian Islands instigated a coup against the ruling Hawaiian queen and established a republic. This cleared the way for U.S. annexation of the islands. President Benjamin Harrison, who strongly advocated this step, justified it this way:

> I think [annexation] will be highly promotive of the best interests of the Hawaiian people, and is the only [step] that will adequately secure the interests of the United States. These interests are not wholly selfish. It is essential that none of the other great powers shall secure these islands. Such a possession would not [be] consist[ent] with our safety and with the peace of the world. [33]

This view eventually prevailed. The process of annexation began in 1898, and two years

Queen Lilioukalani of Hawaii ruled until she was deposed in 1893.

later Hawaii officially became a U.S. territory.

In these same years, the United States acquired a great deal of other territory across the globe. The short but strategically important Spanish-American War, fought in 1898, ended with a resounding Spanish defeat and transferred the last vestiges of Spain's once-great empire to the victor. Through the Treaty of Paris, the United States gained control of Cuba and Puerto Rico, both in the Caribbean region; and Guam and the Philippine Islands in the western Pacific region. Some Filipinos did not like the Americans any better than the Spanish. And it took American troops three years to put down local insurgents in the Philippine-American War (1899–1902).

Japan Learns from the West

Not surprisingly, the new American presence in the Philippines did not go unnoticed by the Japanese, whose home islands lay not far to the north. In fact, at the time that the United States acquired the Philippines, Japan had already begun carving out its own colonial empire. Throughout most of their history, the Japanese had been ardent isolationists, and the concept of aggressive imperialism was new to them. But they learned quickly by observing the Western powers. "Japanese leaders, with their samurai [warrior class] backgrounds, enthusiastically embraced the current imperialism of Europe," noted historian Edwin Reischauer points out. "They saw that poor and small Japan needed more natural resources to become a first-class world power, and they believed that control of adjacent territories would yield many of these resources and strengthen the defenses of Japan."[34]

Among the "adjacent territories" the Japanese coveted was Korea, which had long been controlled by China. In 1894 Japanese troops attacked Chinese soldiers in Korea, initiating the Sino-Japanese War. Japan emerged the clear victor the following year and gained both Korea and the large island of Formosa (present-day Taiwan).

Thus, when the outbreak of World War I in 1914 brought the New Imperialism era to a close, Europe no longer possessed the monopoly on imperialism and colonialism it had once enjoyed. The United States and Japan had boldly asserted their own territorial ambitions. Their gains in the 1890s and early 1900s had proved crucial factors in making both nations world powers. And the Europeans would be forced to reckon with them in the next great round of global colonial activity.

Chapter Six

European Mandates Transform the Middle East

World War I (1914–1918) marked an important turning point in the history of colonialism. During that momentous global conflict, the British, French, Americans, and their allies (collectively termed the Allies) fought against the Germans and their own allies (the Central Powers). Among the Central Powers was the Turkish-run Ottoman Empire, encompassing much of the Middle East. After the Allies defeated the Central Powers, the victors took over many of the losers' colonies around the globe.

These colonies were run under a new system imposed by the League of Nations, an international organization and forerunner of the United Nations created soon after the war's conclusion. The league's system consisted of a series of mandates. A mandate gave a nation the authority to administer a colony as a sort of benevolent caretaker. As the league's charter put it, "There should be applied the principle that the well-being and development of [colo-

nial] peoples form a sacred trust of civilization." The league also recognized that for the time being these colonies "are inhabited by peoples not yet able to stand by themselves under the strenuous conditions of the modern world."[35] There was an understanding that the governing nation would help the colony's inhabitants prepare for independence and self-rule. But no timetables for that process were provided. So it was up to the governing nation to decide when a colony was ready to stand on its own.

With the major exception of Japanese imperialist expansion, which continued apace in eastern Asia, colonial activities in the period between the world wars (1918–1939) were dominated by the mandate system. Particularly crucial were the colonial mandates administered by Britain and France in the Middle East. There, the seeds of a number of new nations were planted. And the events of and mistakes made during this period were profoundly

Delegates of the League of Nations attend their first meeting. The League imposed mandates that allowed Europeans to control the Middle East.

influential in shaping the region's political and cultural landscape for generations to come.

Promises and Betrayal

Even before the outbreak of World War I, some of Europe's great powers jockeyed to gain influence in or control of various parts of the Middle East. The British and French wanted to force the Turks out of the region to reduce the size of and weaken the Ottoman Empire. Also, Britain was worried about increasing German influence in the region, as tensions between the

British and the Germans had been mounting for some time. As Louis L. Snyder explains:

> After several visits to the Turkish sultan, [German leaders] obtained [permission] to construct a railway linking Berlin to Baghdad [in what is now Iraq] and the Persian Gulf. This railway, if completed, would have given Germany access . . . to the rich areas of central and eastern Asia. Britain resolutely opposed the project, which would have . . . been a threat to the

Suez canal, and would have forced a wedge between England and India. British agents put economic pressure on native rulers to prevent the completion of the railway. This issue was undoubtedly a vital factor leading to World War I. [36]

Once the war commenced, the British realized that the natives they had been dealing with in the Middle East could potentially help them drive the Turks and the Germans out of the region. So in 1916, the British, aided by the French, succeeded in briefly uniting a number of the Arab

Lawrence of Arabia

King Faisal, whom the British placed in charge of Iraq, owed much of his success to Britain's T.E. (Thomas Edward) Lawrence, whom both the Arabs and the British came to see as a folk hero. Born in 1888 in Wales, Lawrence attended Jesus College, Oxford, then traveled to the Middle East to pursue a career in archaeology. While there,

he learned Arab language and customs and gained a strong respect for Arab culture. Eventually Lawrence began working for British Military Intelligence, which sent him in 1916 to observe Arab activities during the British-backed Arab revolt. During the next two years he met and became close to Faisal, helped him fight the Turks, and made British officials angry by urging them to grant the Arabs independence. Lawrence's adventures became public and earned him both the nickname Lawrence of Arabia and worldwide fame. His story became the subject of David Lean's movie *Lawrence of Arabia,* which won the Oscar for best picture in 1962.

Thomas Edward Lawrence supported the idea of Arab nationalism.

tribes and organizing them in a revolt against the Turks. This was the first time in centuries that these tribes had achieved any kind of unity. British leaders were successful because they promised the Arabs that if they helped to defeat the Turks, Britain would allow them to establish their own nations in the area. An official document of the period stated:

> The end which France and Great Britain have in view . . . is the complete and definitive liberation of the peoples so long oppressed by the Turks and the establishment of national governments and administrations drawing their authority from the initiative and free choice of indigenous [native] populations. [37]

However, the British and the French did not keep their words. Aided by the Arabs and other local peoples, they were able to drive the Turks out. But after the Allies won the world war, it was revealed that in 1916, at the height of the conflict, Britain and France had concluded a secret pact. Known as the Sykes-Picot Agreement after the names of the men who worked out the deal's details, it provided for the postwar partition and rule of the Middle East by the British and the French. The French would get the northern sector of the region, including Syria, and the British would get the southern sector, including Mesopotamia (Iraq).

When the contents of the Sykes-Picot Agreement became public near the end of the war, Middle Eastern leaders were shocked and saw the deal as a betrayal.

Some reacted by trying to declare their independence and set up new nations in the area. But they had no sizable, organized economies or armies. So they could not stand up to the British and the French, who swiftly put down what these great powers viewed as mere local uprisings. The reality was that Britain and France were now in full control of the Middle East. Still, the natives could take some small consolation from knowing that this colonial takeover was tempered to some degree by the League of Nations' mandate system. British and French officials were forced to assure Arab leaders that various parts of the region would be granted independence in the future.

The British in Iraq

Illustrative of this chain of events and the fate of the mandated colonies was the situation in Mesopotamia, the region that would later become Iraq. In 1920 a group of Iraqi military officers who had long opposed Ottoman rule met in Baghdad. Angry over the broken promises of the British and the French and eager for self-rule, these men declared Iraq to be an independent state. The British immediately moved to put down what they saw as a rebellion against the authority granted to them by their mandate of the region. At the same time, in nearby Syria a prominent Arab leader named Faisal ibn Hussein declared himself to be the king of an independent Syria. A French military force defeated Faisal in July 1920 and forcefully put France's mandate into place in Syria.

These events spawned a great deal of Arab resentment against Britain and

King Faisal (foreground) attends the Versailles peace conference in 1919. T.E. Lawrence stands behind him (second from right).

France as well as a general Arab distrust of European and Western nations. The Arabs and others in the Middle East maintained their anti-European sentiments for many years to come. In addition to being angry over broken promises, they were resentful that Britain, France, and the League of Nations did not view them as capable of governing themselves.

Meanwhile, the British wanted to economically exploit the Middle Eastern territories they held, including Iraq. Howev-

er, they quickly realized that the situation in Iraq was chaotic, with various local groups at odds with one another. Among others, these included Sunni Muslims, Shiite Muslims, and ethnic Kurds. The British decided it would be more to their advantage to let a local leader deal with this potentially volatile situation while maintaining their overall control of the area. They would allow Iraq a measure of sovereignty, as long as its leaders recognized the ultimate superiority of Britain. In this

A photo of Baghdad in 1920, shortly before the arrival of King Faisal. An effective leader, Faisal was able to keep Iraq from falling apart.

way, Iraq would become a protectorate, in essence a colony that could govern itself but would be politically and militarily dependent on its mentor nation.

As for who would rule the protectorate, the British called on Faisal, whom the French had recently defeated in Syria. Thanks to the efforts of his friend, the British adventurer T.E. Lawrence (the famous "Lawrence of Arabia"), after escaping Syria Faisal had found refuge in Britain. In August 1921 the British installed Faisal as king of Iraq. The following year British leaders formalized their protectorate in Iraq through the Anglo-Iraqi Treaty. The agreement stipulated that

Britain would, for the time being, remain in control of Iraq's economic and military affairs. The British also had the right to suspend Iraq's new constitution if they deemed it necessary.

That constitution proved hard to implement, as Faisal encountered difficulty in maintaining local unity and running the country. First, he and his ministers were outsiders because they were Arabs and most of the locals were of Persian descent. Also, Faisal and his aides were Sunni Muslims, who made up a decided minority of Iraq's population. Nevertheless, with British help Faisal managed to keep the country in one piece. And thanks to the discovery of oil there in 1927, Iraq's prosperity increased.

In October 1932 the British mandate over Iraq ended, and Iraq became a full-fledged country, at least in principle. The reality was that Britain had made sure it could maintain a high degree of influence in the area. As part of the agreement that ended the mandate, the Iraqis agreed to sign a treaty giving the British the right to station their military forces in the country for twenty-five years. Thus, though legally independent and no longer a colony, Iraq was still tied to the apron strings of a European nation.

The Palestinian Mandate and Balfour Declaration

Britain also invested a great deal of time, energy, and resources on another of its Middle Eastern mandates—the one for the region of Palestine. There, as in other Middle Eastern areas, British colonial policies created deep resentments both at the time and among later generations. The chief issue of debate and dispute was the desire of the British to create a Jewish homeland in Palestine. To garner Jewish support for their war effort, during World War I Britain negotiated with a group of European Jews known as Zionists. The Zionists advocated that Jews from around the world should be allowed to have their own nation in the Palestinian lands that their ancestors had occupied during biblical times.

The British-Zionist connection came about in the following manner. A noted British chemist named Chaim Weizmann, who was also an ardent Jewish Zionist,

was asked by the British war office to find a way of making synthetic cordite, a potent explosive that would give the British an advantage in the war. After Weizmann succeeded in producing the cordite, many high-ranking British felt beholden to him. It also did not hurt that he possessed a highly persuasive manner and was an excellent public speaker. Weizmann asked British leaders to create a protectorate for a national Jewish homeland in Palestine, and after giving the matter some thought they agreed.

Thus, in November 1917 Lord Balfour, the British foreign secretary, announced the decision of British leaders to help the Jews make a homeland for themselves in the Middle East. His statement became known as the Balfour Declaration. It read in part, "His Majesty's Government views with favor the establishment in Palestine of a national home for the Jewish people, and will use their best endeavors to facilitate the achievement of this object." Trying to sound evenhanded, Balfour added, "Nothing shall be done which may prejudice the civil and religious rights of existing non-Jewish communities in Palestine."[38]

This seemingly simple statement had nothing less than huge implications in the Middle East and elsewhere. When the League of Nations approved the British mandate for Palestine in 1922, it also approved the Balfour Declaration. Many Western nations, including the United States, publicly supported the idea of a Jewish state in Palestine. These countries had large, influential local Jewish communities that pressured their governments to

The Palestinian Mandate

This excerpt from the 1922 League of Nations mandate for Palestine (quoted in volume three of Melvin E. Page's work on colonialism) deals with the creation of a Jewish homeland in Palestine.

The Mandatory [Britain] shall be responsible for placing the country under such political, administrative, and economic conditions as will secure the establishment of the Jewish national home . . . and the development of self-governing institutions, and also for safeguarding the civil and religious rights of all the inhabitants of Palestine, irrespective of race or religion. . . . An appropriate Jewish agency shall be recognized as a public body for the purpose of advising and cooperating with the administration of Palestine in such economic, social, and other matters as may affect the establishment of the Jewish national home and the interests of the Jewish population in Palestine. . . . The Zionist organization . . . shall be recognized as such agency.

Scottish statesman Arthur James Balfour backed the movement for a Jewish homeland in Palestine.

support the Zionists. In response to the declaration, Jews from many parts of the world began moving to the Middle East, believing that the British would eventually grant them an independent nation.

However, many Arabs firmly opposed the creation of a Jewish nation in their midst. In their view, the fact that a majority of people living in the region were Arabs proved that Palestine was an Arab land. They did not care who had occupied the region in ancient times and argued that those who presently lived there had a stronger claim to the land. The Arabs also felt that it was unfair for Britain and the other great powers to deny independence to Arab peoples while helping the Jews create an independent state in the region.

In addition, most Arab leaders interpreted British support for a Jewish homeland as an attempt to gain a Western power base in the region. They worried that British leaders would manipulate the Jewish state behind the scenes. This would supposedly allow Britain to maintain its influence in the area even after the Arabs had managed to gain their independence. Arab bitterness over pro-Zionist British policies marked the beginning of the Arab-Jewish conflict that remains unresolved to this day in the Middle East.

The Oil Factor and U.S. Interests

Independence for Arabs and the question of a Jewish homeland were not the only issues that sparked arguments and deep concerns in the Middle East during the mandate era of colonialism. The existence of plentiful supplies of oil in the region was also a factor affecting the policies of both the locals and the great powers. Both Britain and France desired access to these oil supplies. The 1932 treaty Britain signed with Iraq, whereby the British were allowed to keep troops stationed in Iraq, was partly designed to maintain Britain's access to the rich Iraqi oil fields. The Iraqis and other inhabitants of the Middle East believed that the oil belonged to them. But they also realized that they lacked the money and expertise to extract and refine the oil. So it seemed to make sense, at least

This photo, taken in 1917, shows oil facilities at Basra, near Iraq's Persian Gulf coast. Today, Iraq's oil fields remain rich and productive.

The Father of Israel

Many Israelis recognize that the existence of their nation owes much to Chaim Weizmann, a Jewish chemist, statesman, and Zionist leader. Born in Russia in 1874, Weizmann studied chemistry in Switzerland and became a British citizen in 1910. During World War I he helped the British create more powerful explosives. Also during that conflict, Weizmann lobbied British officials to help the international Zionist movement lay the foundations for a Jewish state in Palestine. In 1920 he became leader of the Zionist movement; and later, after World War II, he obtained U.S. backing for a Jewish state. When that state finally became a reality in 1948, Weizmann served proudly as its first president. He died in 1952.

In 1949 Israel's first president, Dr. Chaim Weizmann, addresses the new nation's first Parliament.

for the time being, to maintain their existing relationships with the European powers.

Another important factor that strongly impacted both oil production and the perpetuation of colonial policies in the Middle East was the entry of the United States into the region. The United States, like Britain and some other Western nations, was becoming increasingly dependent on Middle Eastern oil. Before World War I, the British produced less than 5 percent of the world's oil. However, after occupying the Middle East for a few years after the war, Britain produced more than half of the world's oil. U.S. leaders strongly protested what they viewed as Britain's attempt to corner the world oil market through its exploitation of its colonial protectorates. They reminded British leaders that the Americans had supplied Britain with oil during the great war; therefore, the United States was entitled to a fair share of the abundant oil supplies now being extracted in the Middle Eastern mandated colonies. One American diplomat told his British counterpart, "The United States government believes that it is entitled to participate in any discussions relating to the status of [the Middle Eastern oil] concessions."[39]

The British eventually gave in to U.S. pressure on the oil issue. Britain allowed five U.S. companies to operate in its Iraqi protectorate in 1928. In the years that followed, American oil companies expanded their operations into other Middle Eastern colonial regions, including Kuwait (bordering the Persian Gulf near Iraq), another British protectorate. By 1938 the United States controlled more of the region's oil reserves than any other nation, marking the beginning of American dependence on Middle Eastern oil. Even today, long after these colonial areas became independent nations, the United States remains dependent on their oil. And that dependence has partially shaped U.S. policies in the region, including the U.S. interventions in Iraq in 1991 and 2003. Thus, although the United States had no colonies in the Middle East, it, along with Britain and other powerful nations, has long been, and remains, affected by the colonial policies and ventures of the past.

Chapter Seven

The World Remade: The End of Colonialism

Worldworld War I and its outcome redrew the world's maps and ushered in a new age of colonial enterprise—the era of the mandate system. However, even this mighty upheaval ultimately paled in comparison to the global changes wrought by World War II (1939–1945), by far the most devastating and life-altering conflict in human history. This time the Allies, led by Britain, France, the United States, and the Soviet Union, squared off against the Axis powers— Germany, Italy, and Japan. After six years of incredible strife and bloodshed, the latter three suffered crushing defeats.

One result of the defeat of the Axis countries was that their overseas empires dissolved. Japan, for example, had amassed a huge colonial empire in Southeast Asia in the years between the two world wars. Most of the territories making up this empire had been snatched from the control of Western powers. Now, the inhabitants of these lands were free of the particularly brutal brand of colonial rule imposed by the Japanese. The question was whether they should once more become colonial possessions of the Western powers. In fact, many rejected this route and opted for independence right away.

A prominent example was Vietnam. It had been a part of the French colony of Indochina until Japan conquered it. With Japan out of the picture in 1945, the French tried to reassert their rule in the area. But in September of that year the Vietnamese, led by a local patriot, Ho Chi Minh, issued a declaration of independence based in part on the one that had given birth to the United States in 1776. After condemning both French and Japanese colonial abuses in Vietnam, the document stated:

A people that has courageously opposed French domination for more than eighty years, a people that has fought at the Allies' side these last years against the [Japanese] fascists, such a people must be free, such a people must be independent. [40]

This statement captured a new spirit of self-determination that swept across the globe in the postwar years. It became increasingly clear to people in both the colonies and mother countries that colonialism and imperialism were both outdated and wrong. A man born in one of France's other overseas colonies concisely summed up this view in a speech made in France in 1946: "The process of colonization is ended. . . . No one supports colonization any longer." [41] This sentiment was repeated time and again in the years to come, as one former colony after another became an independent nation. Greatly aiding in this process was the United Nations (UN), a new international organization created in the wake of World War II.

The Era of Colonial Trusts

Partly because the UN was at first completely dominated by the great powers, colonialism did not end abruptly with the formation of that great federation of nations. Most world leaders did realize that the end of old-style colonialism was inevitable. Yet the great powers felt that granting independence to their colonies all at once would be detrimental to both the colonies and the mother countries. The general view was that a transition period was needed to prepare dependent peoples for independent rule.

This was the reasoning behind the UN's so-called trust system, which replaced the old League of Nations mandate system. One major difference between the two sys-

tems was the imposition of timetables. In the case of the mandates, no target dates had been set for granting independence, so, legally speaking, the mother countries had the right to administer their mandates indefinitely. Under the UN trust system, in contrast, the mother countries were required to set target dates. Independence for colonial entities was no longer a mere possibility, providing that various conditions were met, but a certainty. Indeed, the UN Charter, signed by its member nations

Vietnamese patriot Ho Chi Minh opposed French colonial rule of his country.

on June 26, 1945, made it clear that the welfare of colonial peoples, including their eventual independence, was the responsibility of these member nations. Article 73 of the charter reads:

> Members of the United Nations . . . recognize the principle that the interests of the inhabitants of these [dependent] territories are paramount, and accept as a sacred trust the obligation to promote . . . the well-being of the inhabitants of these territories . . . to ensure . . . their just treatment and their protection against abuses . . . [and] to develop self-government [in these colonies] and to assist them in the progressive development of their free political institutions.[42]

The British, who had created the world's largest colonial empire, began this process of freeing their colonies almost immediately. Perhaps the most famous example was India, the most populous colony in the world and long Britain's prize colonial possession. The Indians had indicated their desire for independence long before World War II. In the early decades of the twentieth century, the Indian National Congress, a native political party, assumed leadership of the independence movement. The congress both lobbied and organized protests against Britain. Eventually, Mohandas Gandhi, a former Indi-

Vietnam Declares Independence

The Vietnamese Declaration of Independence (quoted here from Allan B. Cole's Conflict in Indo-China), *issued in September 1945, was based on many of the same ideals and repeated some of the language of the 1776 U.S. version.*

"All men are created equal.". . . This immortal statement was made in the Declaration of Independence of the United States of America. . . . The [French] Declaration [of rights . . . of the French Revolution . . . also states: "All men are born free and with equal rights.". . . Nevertheless, for more than eighty years the French imperialists, deceitfully raising the standard of Liberty, Equality, and Fraternity, have violated our fatherland and opposed our fellow citizens. They have acted contrarily to [against] the ideals of humanity and justice. . . . They have enforced inhuman laws to ruin our unity and national consciousness. . . . They have founded more prisons than schools. They have mercilessly slain our patriots. . . . For these reasons, we, members of the provisional government of Vietnam, declare to the world that Vietnam has the right to be free and independent, and has in fact become a free and independent country.

an lawyer, became the leader of the movement. Both before and during World War II he emphasized peaceful, nonviolent protests as the most ethical and effective means of persuading the British to relinquish control of the country.

British officials initially opposed Gandhi and his movement. But with World War II over and the UN trust system in place, they finally relented and opened a serious dialogue with the Indian National Congress. With both parties working in earnest, preparations for independence proceeded with amazing swiftness and in August 1947 India became a sovereign nation. At the same time, per an agreement worked out with Britain, two sections of the former colony became East and West Pakistan, to be inhabited and governed by Indian Muslims.

This process was repeated across the globe in the late 1940s and into the 1950s. And as more and more colonies gained independence, they joined the UN, which, in turn, had the effect of accelerating the implementation of the organization's trust system. John W. Cell explains, "After achieving independence and becoming members of the U.N. . . . several former colonies led a campaign against colonialism. . . . In this way, trusteeship accelerated the movement toward decolonization throughout the world."[43]

Colonialism Begins to Collapse

Thus, colonialism as a global phenomenon rapidly began to collapse. The naked imperialism that had created the colonial empires in the first place was also on the

Gandhi visits 10 Downing Street, residence of the British prime minister, in 1931.

wane. There were some glaring exceptions to this rule, however. For four decades following World War II, the Soviet Union used force to maintain control over Poland, Hungary, Latvia, and other eastern European states, all of which desired freedom. They eventually gained their independence when the Soviet Union collapsed in 1991.

The Goals of the UN Trust System

The United Nations Trust (or, more formally, "Trusteeship") system was set up in the wake of World War II. This excerpt from Article 75 of the UN Charter (quoted in volume three of Page's Colonialism*) lays out the system's goals.*

To further international peace and security; to promote the political, economic, social, and educational advancement of the inhabitants of the trust territories, and their progressive development towards self-government or independence. . . . To encourage respect for human rights and for fundamental freedoms for all [peoples] without distinction as to race, sex, language, or religion, and to encourage recognition of the interdependence of the peoples of the world.

In the West, meanwhile, a last gasp of the old imperialist-colonial mindset surfaced in the so-called Suez crisis. In 1952 a group of Egyptian army officers overthrew the corrupt government of King Farouk, the British-backed ruler of the country. Four years later, the new president, Gamal Abdel Nasser, seized control of the Suez Canal. He declared that it belonged to Egypt, not the British and the French who had long administered it. Britain and France sent troops to invade Egypt and retake the canal. But though this military action was largely successful, it was soon unexpectedly nullified by a third party. Upholding the growing anticolonial spirit around the world, the United States forced the British and French to withdraw. Historians came to see this momentous event as the symbolic end of the British Empire and the moment when the world realized that the United States had replaced Britain as the leading Western superpower.

Britain's failure to hold onto the canal was only one of many examples of the disintegration of the old colonial empires, including its own. In Africa in 1957, only a year after the Suez crisis, Ghana, formerly the British Gold Coast colony, became an independent nation. It was the first black African state to break free of European colonial rule. The following year Ghana's leader, Kwame Nkrumah, organized the All-African People's Conference to promote and facilitate the decolonization of other African states. The conference issued a resolution on colonialism and imperialism that stated in part:

The All-African People's Conference vehemently condemns colonialism and imperialism in whatever shape or form these evils are perpetrated. The political and economic exploitation of Africans by imperialist Europeans should cease forthwith. . . .

Fundamental human rights [should] be extended to all men and women in Africa. . . . Universal adult franchise [voting rights] [should] be extended to all persons in Africa regardless of race or sex. [44]

Within twelve years of the writing of these words, the vast majority of former African colonies had become independent nations.

In the meantime, decolonization continued throughout the 1940s, 1950s, and 1960s in other parts of the world. To name only a few, the Philippines gained independence from the United States in 1946; the island of Ceylon off India's eastern coast became independent of Britain in 1948 and took the name Sri Lanka in 1972; the Dutch East Indies acquired independence from the Netherlands and became the nation of Indonesia in 1949; Cambodia became independent of France in 1953; in 1962 Jamaica in the Caribbean became free of British control; also in 1962 Samoa in the Pacific was granted independence by New Zealand; and in 1964 Malta in the Mediterranean gained independence from Britain. As Louis L. Snyder aptly puts it, "The whole edifice of world imperialism seemed to collapse in [only a few] short years, certainly one of the most sudden transformations in the history of civilization." [45]

Democracy Sweeps the World

As the collapse of colonialism proceeded, the world was remade not only through the spread of sovereignty and self-rule in former colonies. The second half of the twentieth century also witnessed a dramatic transformation in the manner in which many of these states were governed. A majority of new independent nations that rose from the wreckage of the colonial empires chose to institute democracy.

Ironically, this was one example of the imperialist countries imparting something decidedly positive to the lands they had once controlled. Britain's system of parliamentary democracy became a model copied by numerous emerging nations around the globe. Also highly influential were the democratic ideals and writings that had emerged from the American and French revolutions, including the U.S. Declaration of Independence (1776) and French Declaration of the Rights of Man and of the Citizen (1789).

These democratic influences were felt not only in the new constitutions of many of the former colonies but also in the charter of the United Nations, in which each of these states now had a voice. The UN Charter contains a declaration of rights based, to various degrees, on the U.S. Declaration of Independence and Bill of Rights, the French Declaration, and the English Bill of Rights (1689). "All human beings are born free and equal in dignity and rights," the UN declaration begins.

They are endowed with reason and conscience and should act towards one another in a spirit of brotherhood. . . . Everyone is entitled to all the rights and freedoms set forth in this declaration, without distinction of any kind, such as race, color, sex, language, religion, political or other opinion, national or social origin, property, birth, or other status. [46]

Such words typified the spirit of the men and women who crafted the numerous new democratic governments that sprang up far and wide in the wake of colonialism's collapse. Indeed, their sheer number was remarkable. For the first time in history democracy became the leading form of government in the world. Before the American Revolution in 1776, no democracies existed. By 1950, 22 countries had democratic governments, encompassing about 31 percent of the world's population. These numbers increased with amazing rapidity in the ensuing decades. Today, 121 of the world's 194 independent nations have democratic systems, although some grant their citizens more civil rights than others do.

The rising tide of independence and democracy among the world's former colonies also ensured that any future attempts to establish colonial empires would be difficult at best. In 1960, influenced by this tide, the UN roundly condemned colonialism, saying:

> The subjection of peoples to alien [outside] subjugation, domination, and exploitation constitutes a denial of fundamental human rights, is contrary to the Charter of the United Nations, and is an impediment to the promotion of world peace and cooperation. [47]

Though forceful, this statement gave the UN no legal authority to stop colonial practices. Only ten years later, however, the UN took the final, bold step and made such practices an international crime.

The Mixed Legacy of Colonialism and Imperialism

Thus, independence and the spread of democracy and human rights proved to be positive aspects of the massive legacy of the age of colonialism. Other benefits gained by many of the former colonies in the twentieth century included increased access to advanced technology and improved health care. Yet historians and other knowledgeable observers caution that colonialism's legacy had many negative aspects as well. One of the most prominent is lingering racial, religious, and cultural intolerance. As Cell explains it:

> White settlers who conquered non-white peoples often held the attitude that ethnic and cultural differences define some people as superior and others as inferior. Some colonizing countries began education programs that maintained white superiority by distancing native students from their own culture and history. [48]

One result of these practices was that, even after gaining independence and instituting democracy, some former colonies still must deal with racial and/or religious tensions within their own societies.

Also, the age of colonialism left behind a legacy of violence in a number of new nations that have found it difficult to settle local differences and disputes, most of which originated in the colonial era. Such disputes have led some former colonies to make war on their neighbors, as when Iraq invaded Kuwait in 1990. Similarly, civil wars and genocidal policies continue to

The Creation of the State of Israel

Among the many new nations that arose in former colonial regions after World War II was Israel. This is an excerpt from that country's Proclamation of Independence (quoted in Snyder's Imperialism Reader*), issued on May 14, 1948.*

On November 29, 1947, the General Assembly of the United Nations adopted a resolution requiring the establishment of a Jewish state in Palestine. . . . It is the natural right of the Jewish people to lead, as do all other nations, an independent existence in its sovereign state. Accordingly, we, the members of the National Council, representing the Jewish people in Palestine and the World Zionist Movement, are met together in solemn assembly today, the day of termination of the British Mandate for Palestine; and by virtue of the natural and historic right of the Jewish people and the Resolution of the General Assembly of the United Nations, we hereby proclaim the establishment of the Jewish State of Palestine, to be called Medinath Yisrael (The State of Israel).

On May 14, 1948, Prime Minister David Ben-Gurion reads Israel's statement of independence to gathered Israeli officials.

A mass grave is prepared for the victims of genocide in Democratic Republic of Congo, formerly a European colony (the Belgian Congo), in the early 1990s.

ravage some former colonies, especially in Africa. One of the worst of the civil conflicts is the second one fought in the Sudan, in North Africa, since it became independent; between 1983 and 2005, almost 2 million people were killed and another 4 million became homeless. As Bonnie G. Smith points out:

> It is one of imperialism's [and colonialism's] many paradoxes that while it made people more aware than ever before of the world's multiple races, accomplishments, and cultures, it set a trend of pitting humans against one another in an orgy of conquest, competition, and hatred. [49]

The legacy of colonialism therefore has been mixed. All of the former colonies have both benefited and suffered from their relationships with the former imperialist nations. Only the passage of time will show whether the benefits will ultimately heal and erase the effects and memories of the suffering. For the present, Smith adds, people in all nations must recognize the reality that, though colonialism and imperialism are no longer openly practiced, they "continue to shape our present world." [50]

Notes

Introduction: The Failure to Learn from History

1. George Santayana, *The Life of Reason,* vol. 1. New York: Scribner's, 1905, p. 284.
2. Louis L. Snyder, ed., *The Imperialism Reader.* Port Washington, NY: Kennikat, 1973, p. 3.
3. Snyder, *The Imperialism Reader,* p. 1.

Chapter One: The First Great Age of Colonialism

4. William H. McNeill, *The Rise of the West.* Chicago: University of Chicago Press, 1992, pp. 619–20.
5. John W. Cell, "Colonialism and Colonies," Encarta Online Encyclopedia, 2005, pp. 7–8. http://encarta.msn.com/encyclopedia_761576293/Colonialism_and_Colonies.html.
6. Quoted in Howard Zinn, *A People's History of the United States.* New York: HarperCollins, 1990, p. 1.
7. McNeill, *The Rise of the West,* p. 628.
8. Eric A. Jones, "The Dutch Empire," in *Colonialism,* vol. 1, ed. Melvin E. Page. Santa Barbara, CA: ABC-CLIO, 2003, p. 174.
9. Quoted in James H. Robinson, ed., *Readings in European History,* 2 vols. Boston: Ginn, 1904–1906, pp. 333–34.

Chapter Two: The Challenges of Running a Colony

10. Cell, "Colonialism and Colonies," p. 11.
11. Cell, "Colonialism and Colonies," p. 14.
12. Zinn, *A People's History of the United States,* p. 21.
13. Arthur de Gobineau, *The Inequality of Human Races,* trans. Adrian Collins. New York: Putnam, 1915, pp. 205–10.
14. Lauren A. Kattner, "Indentured Servitude," in *Colonialism,* vol. 2, ed. Melvin E. Page. Santa Barbara, CA: ABC-CLIO, 2003, p. 524.
15. Alan K. Smith, *Creating a World Economy: Merchant Capital, Colonialism, and World Trade, 1400–1825.* San Francisco: Westview, 1991, p. 177.

Chapter Three: Early Resistance to Colonialism

16. Cell, "Colonialism and Colonies," p. 32.
17. Quoted in Henry S. Commager and Richard B. Morris, eds., *The Spirit of 'Seventy-six: The Story of the American Revolution as Told by Participants,* vol. 1. New York: Bobbs-Merrill, 1958, p. 39.
18. Simón Bolívar, *An Address of Bolívar at the Congress of Angostura.* Washington, DC: B.S. Adams, 1919, p. 5.
19. Quoted in Sons of DeWitt Colony Texas, "Mexican Independence." www.tamu.edu/ccbn/dewitt/mexicanrev.htm#hidalgo.
20. Quoted in *Workers' Liberty,* "The Haitian Revolution and Atlantic Slavery." http://archive.workersliberty.org/wlmags/wl102/haiti.htm.

Chapter Four: "The Sun Never Sets": Britain's Empire Expands

21. Snyder, *The Imperialism Reader*, p. 1.
22. Robert Y. Eng, "China," in *Colonialism*, vol. 1, ed. Melvin E. Page. Santa Barbara, CA: ABC-CLIO, 2003, p. 113.
23. John Stuart Mill, "On Colonies and Colonization," in *Principles of Political Economy*, ed. J.L. Laughlan. New York: D. Appleton, 1891, pp. 543–44.
24. Quoted in Snyder, *The Imperialism Reader*, pp. 87–88.
25. Snyder, *The Imperialism Reader*, p. 9.
26. Evelyn Baring, *Modern Egypt*, vol. 2. New York: Macmillan, 1908, p. 46.
27. Huang Chueh Tz'u, "The Evil of Opium," in *China in Transition, 1517–1911*, ed. Dun J. Li. New York: Van Nostrand Reinhold, 1969, p. 55.

Chapter Five: The New Imperialism and Scramble for Africa

28. Cell, "Colonialism and Colonies," p. 29.
29. Quoted in *Daily Telegraph* (London), October 22, 1884.
30. Quoted in *Times* (London), January 11, 1876.
31. Thomas Pakenham, *The Scramble for Africa*. New York: Random House, 1991, p. xxiii.
32. Robert W. July, *A History of the African People*. Long Grove, IL: Waveland, 1997, p. 320.
33. Quoted in Henry S. Commager, *Documents in American History*, vol. 1. Englewood Cliffs, NJ: Prentice-Hall, 1973, pp. 602–603.
34. Edwin Reischauer, *Japan: Past and Present*. New York: Knopf, 1964, p. 135.

Chapter Six: European Mandates Transform the Middle East

35. Covenant of the League of Nations, Section 22. www.rmc.ca/academic/gradrech/UNCharter-LeagueCov.doc.
36. Snyder, *The Imperialism Reader*, pp. 10–11.
37. Quoted in Bonnie G. Smith, ed., *Imperialism: A History in Documents*. New York: Oxford University Press, 2000, p. 141.
38. Quoted in Snyder, *The Imperialism Reader*, p. 376.
39. Quoted in *Papers Relating to the Foreign Relations of the United States, 1920*, vol. 11. Washington, DC: Government Printing Office, 1936, p. 655.

Chapter Seven: The World Remade: The End of Colonialism

40. Quoted in Allan B. Cole, ed., *Conflict in Indo-China and International Repercussions, a Documentary History, 1945–1955*. Ithaca, NY: Cornell University Press, 1956, p. 21.
41. Quoted in Snyder, *The Imperialism Reader*, p. 492.
42. Quoted in Page, *Colonialism*, vol. 3, p. 1019.
43. Cell, "Colonialism and Colonies," p. 30.
44. Quoted in Page, *Colonialism*, vol. 3, p. 1039.
45. Snyder, *The Imperialism Reader*, p. 12.
46. Quoted in Diane Ravitch and Abigail Thernstrom, eds., *The Democracy Reader*. New York: HarperCollins, 1992, pp. 202–203.
47. Quoted in Page, *Colonialism*, vol. 3, p. 1049.
48. Cell, "Colonialism and Colonies," p. 31.
49. Smith, *Imperialism*, pp. 164–65.
50. Smith, *Imperialism*, p. 165.

For Further Reading

Books

Mark A. Burkholder and Lyman L. Johnson, *Colonial Latin America.* New York: Oxford University Press, 2003. A comprehensive but easy-to-read look at Europe's colonization and exploitation of Latin America.

Terry Deary, *The Barmy British Empire.* New York: Scholastic, 2002. Much relevant information is here presented in a light-hearted manner.

Sarah Flowers, *The Age of Exploration.* San Diego: Lucent, 1999. A well-written synopsis of the European nations and explorers who arrived in and began colonizing distant parts of the world in the 1500s and 1600s.

Don Nardo, *Modern Japan.* San Diego: Lucent, 1995. Provides information about Japanese imperialism and colonial efforts in southeast Asia in the early twentieth century.

Jonathan T. Reynolds and Erik Gilbert, *Africa in World History.* New York: Prentice Hall, 2003. An easy-to-read overview of African history, including European colonial policy in the area.

Web Sites

The British Presence in India in the Eighteenth Century (www.bbc.co.uk/history/state/empire/east_india_01.shtml) Sponsored by the British Broadcasting Company, this is a fine overview of how the British got involved in India.

Colonial Powers and the Colonized (www.fsmitha.com/h2/ch23t.htm). This site covers French colonialism in Algeria and Vietnam, the colonization of Indonesia by the Dutch, and the Americans in the Philippines.

European Imperialism, 1851–1900 (www.fsmitha.com/h3/h50.htm). This Web site covers resistance to colonialism in many parts of the world in the late 1800s and the twentieth century.

Works Consulted

Major Works

David Cannandine, *How the British Saw Their Empire.* New York: Oxford University Press, 2002. An excellent scholarly examination of British imperialism.

Arthur de Gobineau, *The Inequality of the Human Race.* Trans. Adrian Collins. New York: Putnam, 1915.

James L. Gelvin, *The Modern Middle East: A History.* New York: Oxford University Press, 2004. One of the best recent studies of the turbulent affairs of the countries of the Middle East, including Iran, Iraq, Syria, Saudi Arabia, and others.

Eric Hobsbawm, *The Age of Empire, 1875–1914.* New York: Pantheon, 1987. An excellent overview of the major events, players, and themes of the New Imperialism era.

Henry Kamen, *How Spain Became a World Power, 1492–1763.* New York: Harper, 2004. A comprehensive and engaging examination of Spanish colonization and imperialism.

Ramon Myers and Mark R. Peattie, *The Japanese Colonial Empire, 1895–1945.* Princeton, NJ: Princeton University Press, 1984. This comprehensive study traces the background and events of Japanese expansion and concludes with Japan's defeat at the end of World War II.

Melvin E. Page, *Colonialism.* 3 Vols. Santa Barbara, CA: ABC-CLIO, 2003. The most comprehensive general overview of the subject presently available. The articles are generally short, but many are informative.

Thomas Pakenham, *The Scramble for Africa.* New York: Random House, 1991. This huge tome is seen by many as the definitive modern study of European colonialism in Africa.

J.H. Parry, *Trade and Dominion: The European Overseas Empires in the Eighteenth Century.* New York: Sterling, 2001. A well-researched, somewhat scholarly synopsis of French, British, and other European colonialism in the 1700s.

Alan K. Smith, *Creating a World Economy: Merchant Capital, Colonialism, and World Trade, 1400–1825.* San Francisco: Westview, 1991. This volume examines the economic factors that affected global colonialism over the course of more than four centuries.

Daniel Yergin, *The Prize: The Epic Quest for Oil, Money, and Power.* New York: Simon and Schuster, 1993. Winner of the Pulitzer Prize, this is a penetrating look at the history of the modern oil industry and how rich nations and companies have exploited oil resources in smaller countries around the world.

Other Important Works

Primary Sources

Evelyn Baring, *Modern Egypt.* Vol. 2. New York: Macmillan, 1908.

Leon Bernard and Theodore B. Hodges, eds., *Readings in European History.* New York: Macmillan, 1958.

Simón Bolívar, *An Address of Bolívar at the Congress of Angostura.* Washington, DC: B.S. Adams, 1919.

Allan B. Cole, ed., *Conflict in Indo-China and International Repercussions, a Documentary History, 1945–1955.* Ithaca, NY: Cornell University Press, 1956.

Henry S. Commager, *Documents in American History.* Vol. 1. Englewood Cliffs, NJ: Prentice-Hall, 1973.

Henry S. Commager and Richard B. Morris, eds., *The Spirit of 'Seventy-six: The Story of the American Revolution as Told by Participants.* Vol. 1. New York: Bobbs-Merrill, 1958.

Basil Davidson, ed., *African Civilization Revisited.* Trenton, NJ: Africa World, 1991.

Thomas Jefferson, *Summary View of the Rights of British America.* In *Thomas Jefferson: Writings.* Ed. Merrill D. Peterson. New York: Library of America, 1984.

Dun J. Li, ed., *China in Transition, 1517–1911.* New York: Van Nostrand Reinhold, 1969.

John Stuart Mill, *Principles of Political Economy.* Ed. J.L. Laughlan. New York: D. Appleton, 1891.

Samuel E. Morison, ed., *Sources and Documents Illustrating the American Revolution, 1764–1788, and the Formation of the Federal Constitution.* Oxford, England: Clarendon, 1953.

Papers Relating to the Foreign Relations of the United States, 1920. Vol. 11. Washington, DC: Government Printing Office, 1936.

Diane Ravitch and Abigail Thernstrom, eds., *The Democracy Reader.* New York: HarperCollins, 1992.

James H. Robinson, ed., *Readings in European History.* 2 Vols. Boston: Ginn, 1904–1906.

Bonnie G. Smith, ed., *Imperialism: A History in Documents.* New York: Oxford University Press, 2000.

Louis L. Snyder, ed., *The Imperialism Reader.* Port Washington, NY: Kennikat, 1973.

Modern Sources
Books

Ludwig Bauer, *Leopold the Unloved.* Boston: Little, Brown, 1935.

O. Nigel Bolland, *Struggles for Freedom: Essays on Slavery, Colonialism, and Culture in the Caribbean and Central America.* Belize City, Belize: Angelus, 1997.

J.H. Elliott, *Imperial Spain, 1469–1716.* Berkeley and Los Angeles: University of California Press, 1990.

Robert W. July, *A History of the African People.* Long Grove, IL: Waveland, 1997.

George Lichtheim, *Imperialism.* New York: Praeger, 1971.

W.M. Roger Louis, ed., *The Oxford History of the British Empire.* 5 vols. New York: Oxford University Press, 1998–1999.

Marlene J. Mayo, ed., *The Emergence of Imperial Japan.* Lexington, MA: Heath, 1970.

William H. McNeill, *The Rise of the West.* Chicago: University of Chicago Press, 1992.

Frederick Quinn, *The French Overseas Empire.* Westport, CT: Praeger, 2000.

Edwin Reischauer, *Japan: Past and Present.* New York: Knopf, 1964.

George Santayana, *The Life of Reason.* Vol. 1. New York: Scribner's, 1905.

Wilcomb E. Washburn, ed., *The Indian and the White Man.* Garden City, NY: Doubleday, 1964.

Harrison M. Wright, ed., *The "New Imperialism."* Boston: D.C. Heath, 1976.

Howard Zinn, *A People's History of the United States.* New York: HarperCollins, 1990.

Internet Sources

Simón Bolívar, "Proclamation to the People of Venezuela," June 15, 1813. www.geocities.com/Athens/Acropolis/7609/eng/bolivar/venezuela1813.html.

John W. Cell, "Colonialism and Colonies," Encarta Online Encyclopedia, 2005. http://encarta.msn.com/encyclopedia_761576293/Colonialism_and_Colonies.html.

Covenant of the League of Nations, Section 22. www.rmc.ca/academic/gradrech/UNCharter-LeagueCov.doc.

Mogamat G. Kamedien, "Slavery at the Cape: The Cape Slave Code of 1754." http://batavia.rug.ac.be/slavery/code1754.htm.

Joseph V. O'Brien, "Imperialism: Sample of Native Treaty." http://web.jjay.cuny.edu/~jobrien/reference/ob43.html.

Sons of DeWitt Colony Texas, "Mexican Independence." www.tamu.edu/ccbn/dewitt/mexicanrev.htm#hidalgo.

United Nations, "Resolutions Adopted by the General Assembly During Its 25th Season." www.un.org/documents/ga/res/25/ares25.htm.

Workers' Liberty, "The Haitian Revolution and Atlantic Slavery," http://archive.workersliberty.org/wlmags/wl1102/haiti.htm.

Web Sites

Avalon Project of the Yale Law School, www.yale.edu/lawweb/avalon/avalon.htm. A large collection of primary source documents.

Index

Clemens, Samuel, 68
coal, 63
Coercive Acts, 42–43
coffee, 22, 26, 32, 46
Colombia, 45
colonialism, 10–11
    beginnings of, 13, 16–27
    end of, 15, 82–87
    legacy of, 12–13, 51–54, 56–57, 88–90
    nineteenth century, 14, 61–70
    resistance to, 39–49
colonies, 10–11, 19, 28–38
    see also specific locations and types of colonies
colonists. *See grachupines; mestizos; whites*
Columbus, Christopher, 13, 18, 19–20, 22, 27, 35
competition, 19, 22, 24, 50, 58, 61, 90
    see also wars
Congo Free State, 64, 66–68
contested settlement colonies, 29
conversion, 19, 37, 54, 55
copper, 61, 63
cordite, 77
cotton, 24, 26, 28, 63
Creoles/criolles, 45
crops, 28, 46
Cuba, 18, 20, 36, 69
culture, 35, 55, 88

Declaration of Independence (U.S.), 41, 82, 84, 87
Declaration of the Rights of Man and of the Citizen (France), 87
democracy, 87–88
dependent territories, 11, 15, 63, 84
Dias, Batholomew, 22
discrimination. See racism
Dutch, 22–25, 34, 36, 50
Dutch East India Company, 22–23
Dutch East Indies, 87
Dutty, Boukman, 47

dyes, 24

Eastern Europe, 85
economics, 19, 32–33, 38, 51
Ecuador, 45
effective occupation, 65–66
Egypt, 51, 57–58, 60, 86
empires, 10–16, 19, 21, 34, 50–61, 68
England/English, 45, 82
    African colonies of, 66
    empire of, 10–16, 50–61, 68
    India as colony of, 24–25, 28–29, 51–59
    loss of colonies by, 39–43, 84–87
    Middle Eastern colonies of, 71–81
    North American colonies of, 28, 30–32, 34, 36, 54
Europe/Europeans
    African colonies of, 61–70
    empires of, 12–28, 50
    loss of colonies by, 38–49, 86
    racism of, 34–36, 54
    see also Eastern Europe; *and individual countries*
expansion, 16–18, 39, 54, 61, 71
exploitation, 16, 20, 36–38, 56, 61, 63–64
    of colonies, 28, 30–34, 40, 46–49
exploration, 16–27
exports, 19, 24–25, 32

fabrics, 19
    see also specific fabrics
Faisal ibn Hussein (king of Iraq), 73–74, 76
Far East, 20, 22, 24, 39
Farouk (king of Egypt), 86
First Opium War, 58
Florida, 20
Force Publique (FP), 66
Formosa, 70
France/French, 13, 16, 18, 24, 57
    African colonies of, 26–27, 36, 61, 66
    Caribbean colonies of, 31–32, 38, 40

tariffs, 32
taxes, 13, 32, 40–43
tea, 24, 32, 42
telegraph, 63
timber, 18, 19, 32
tin, 59, 61
tobacco, 26
Toussaint-Louverture, 47–49
trade, 19–20, 22–24, 38–39, 51, 56, 58
treaties, 51, 63, 65
Treaty of Nanking, 58
Treaty of Paris, 69
tropical dependencies, 28, 30–34, 40,
46–49
trust system, 83–86
Turkey/Turks, 14, 71, 73–74
Twain, Mark. *See* Clemens, Samuel

United Nations (UN), 15, 71, 83–85,
87–89
United States
formation of, 11, 39–43, 46, 82
imperialism of, 14–15, 54, 61, 68–70
loss of colonies by, 87
Middle East policy of, 14–15, 71, 77,
79–81, 86

Venezuela, 21, 41, 43–45

Vietnam, 82–84
Vikings, 19
violence. *See* genocide; wars
Virginia, 10, 25, 26, 30–31
Virginia Company, 26
Voodoo, 47

war on terrorism, 15
wars, 31, 38–39, 64–65, 88
see also rebellions; *and specific revolutions and wars*
wealth, 19, 38, 53
Weizmann, Chaim, 77, 80
West Indies, 13, 18, 19, 32
"White Man's Burden, The" (Kipling),
52, 53–54, 63
whites, 12–13, 29, 40
domination by, 31–36, 46–47, 53–58,
60, 63, 88
women, 23
wool, 32
World War I, 70–74, 81
World War II, 15, 82–83

Yoruba (tribe), 47

Zimbabwe, 29
Zionists, 77–80, 89

Picture Credits

Cover: © Michael Maslin Historic Photography/CORBIS

Akg-images, 55, 57

Associated Press/AP, 90

Biblarchive Preussischer Kulturebesitz/ Art Resource, N.Y., 21

Giraudon/Art Resource, N.Y., 56

HIP/Art Resource, N.Y., 53

Bridgeman Art Library, 40, 46

© Archivo Iconografico,S.A., 8 (lower right)

© Bettmann/CORBIS, 9 (lower right), 11, 14, 24-25, 41, 42, 59, 65, 69, 73, 75, 76, 80, 89

© Christies' Images/CORBIS, 44

© Olivier Coret/In Visu/CORBIS, 15

© Hulton-Deutsch Collection/CORBIS, 52, 72, 79, 83, 85

© Michael Nicholson/CORBIS, 60, 78

© Poodlesrock/CORBIS, 8 (upper left)

© Stapleton Collection/CORBIS, 64

Hulton Archive by Getty Images, 23, 30

Courtesy of the Hebrew University of Jerusalem, 9 (upper right)

Library of Congress, 9 (lower left)

Mary Evans Picture Library, 35, 67

North Wind Picture Archives, 8 (lower left), 12, 17, 18, 20, 29, 33, 37, 48

About the Author

In addition to his acclaimed volumes on the ancient world, historian Don Nardo has written and edited many books for young adults about modern history and government, including *The French Revolution, The Mexican-American War, The Declaration of Independence, The Bill of Rights, The Great Depression,* and *World War II in the Pacific.* Mr. Nardo also writes screenplays and teleplays and composes music. He lives with his wife, Christine, in Massachusetts.